An Analysis of

Hanna Batatu's

The Old Social Classes and the Revolutionary Movements of Iraq

Dale J. Stahl

Published by Macat International Ltd
24:13 Coda Centre, 189 Munster Road, London SW6 6AW.

Distributed exclusively by Routledge
2 Park Square, Milton Park, Abingdon, Oxon OX14 4RN
711 Third Avenue, New York, NY 10017, USA

Routledge is an imprint of the Taylor & Francis Group, an informa business

www.macat.com
info@macat.com

Cataloguing in Publication Data
A catalogue record for this book is available from the British Library.
Library of Congress Cataloguing-in-Publication Data is available upon request.
Cover illustration:Etienne Gilfillan

ISBN 978-1-912302-44-4 (hardback)
ISBN 978-1-912128-45-7 (paperback)
ISBN 978-1-912281-32-9 (e-book)

Notice
The information in this book is designed to orientate readers of the work under analysis,
to elucidate and contextualise its key ideas and themes, and to aid in the development
of critical thinking skills. It is not meant to be used, nor should it be used, as a
substitute for original thinking or in place of original writing or research. References and
notes are provided for informational purposes and their presence does not constitute
endorsement of the information or opinions therein. This book is presented solely for
educational purposes. It is sold on the understanding that the publisher is not engaged
to provide any scholarly advice. The publisher has made every effort to ensure that
this book is accurate and up-to-date, but makes no warranties or representations with
regard to the completeness or reliability of the information it contains. The information
and the opinions provided herein are not guaranteed or warranted to produce particular
results and may not be suitable for students of every ability. The publisher shall not be
liable for any loss, damage or disruption arising from any errors or omissions, or from
the use of this book, including, but not limited to, special, incidental, consequential or
other damages caused, or alleged to have been caused, directly or indirectly, by the
information contained within.

CONTENTS

THE MACAT LIBRARY

The Macat Library is a series of unique academic explorations of seminal works in the humanities and social sciences – books and papers that have had a significant and widely recognised impact on their disciplines. It has been created to serve as much more than just a summary of what lies between the covers of a great book. It illuminates and explores the influences on, ideas of, and impact of that book. Our goal is to offer a learning resource that encourages critical thinking and fosters a better, deeper understanding of important ideas.

Each publication is divided into three Sections: Influences, Ideas, and Impact. Each Section has four Modules. These explore every important facet of the work, and the responses to it.

This Section-Module structure makes a Macat Library book easy to use, but it has another important feature. Because each Macat book is written to the same format, it is possible (and encouraged!) to cross-reference multiple Macat books along the same lines of inquiry or research. This allows the reader to open up interesting interdisciplinary pathways.

To further aid your reading, lists of glossary terms and people mentioned are included at the end of this book (these are indicated by an asterisk [*] throughout) – as well as a list of works cited.

Macat has worked with the University of Cambridge to identify the elements of critical thinking and understand the ways in which six different skills combine to enable effective thinking.
Three allow us to fully understand a problem; three more give us the tools to solve it. Together, these six skills make up the **PACIER** model of critical thinking. They are:

ANALYSIS – understanding how an argument is built
EVALUATION – exploring the strengths and weaknesses of an argument
INTERPRETATION – understanding issues of meaning

CREATIVE THINKING – coming up with new ideas and fresh connections
PROBLEM-SOLVING – producing strong solutions
REASONING – creating strong arguments

To find out more, visit **WWW.MACAT.COM.**

CRITICAL THINKING AND *THE OLD SOCIAL CLASSES AND THE REVOLUTIONARY MOVEMENTS OF IRAQ*

Primary critical thinking skill: PROBLEM-SOLVING
Secondary critical thinking skill: REASONING

How do you solve a problem like understanding Iraq? For Hanna Batatu, the solution to this conundrum lay in generating alternative possibilities that effectively side-stepped the conventional wisdom of the time.

Historians had long held that Iraq – like other artificial creations of ex-colonial European powers, who drew lines onto the world map that ignored longstanding tribal, ethnic and religious ties – was best understood by delving into its political and religious history. Batatu used the problem solving skills of asking productive questions and generating alternative possibilities to argue that Iraq's history was better understood through the lens of a Marxist analysis focused on socio-economic history.

The Old Social Classes concludes that the divisions present in Iraq – and exposed by the revolutionary movements of the 1950s – are those characterized by the struggle for control over property and the means of production. Additionally, Batatu sought to establish that the most important political movements of the time, notably the nationalist Ba'athists and the pan-Arab Free Officers Movement, had their origins in a homegrown communist ideology inspired by local conditions and local inequality. By posing new questions – and by undertaking a vast amount of research in primary sources, a rarity in the history of this region – Batatu was able to produce a strong, new solution to a longstanding historiographical puzzle.

ABOUT THE AUTHOR OF THE ORIGINAL WORK

Hanna Batatu was born in Jerusalem, Palestine, in 1926 and left for the United States after the 1948 Arab-Israeli war. He became an academic, specializing in Iraq, its politics and its history. Returning to the Middle East for research, Batatu lived in Lebanon for 20 years—until Israel invaded in 1982, at which point he returned to the US to teach at Harvard. Batatu experienced the turmoil of the region over decades and witnessed the rise of Arab nationalism. He died in 2000, aged 74, in Connecticut.

ABOUT THE AUTHOR OF THE ANALYSIS

Dr Dale Stahl holds a doctorate in history from Columbia University for research on the politics of Iraq between 1920 and 1975. He currently teaches in the College of Liberal Arts and Sciences at the University of Denver, Colorado.

ABOUT MACAT

GREAT WORKS FOR CRITICAL THINKING

Macat is focused on making the ideas of the world's great thinkers accessible and comprehensible to everybody, everywhere, in ways that promote the development of enhanced critical thinking skills.

It works with leading academics from the world's top universities to produce new analyses that focus on the ideas and the impact of the most influential works ever written across a wide variety of academic disciplines. Each of the works that sit at the heart of its growing library is an enduring example of great thinking. But by setting them in context – and looking at the influences that shaped their authors, as well as the responses they provoked – Macat encourages readers to look at these classics and game-changers with fresh eyes. Readers learn to think, engage and challenge their ideas, rather than simply accepting them.

'Macat offers an amazing first-of-its-kind tool for interdisciplinary learning and research. Its focus on works that transformed their disciplines and its rigorous approach, drawing on the world's leading experts and educational institutions, opens up a world-class education to anyone.'

Andreas Schleicher
Director for Education and Skills, Organisation for Economic Co-operation and Development

'Macat is taking on some of the major challenges in university education … They have drawn together a strong team of active academics who are producing teaching materials that are novel in the breadth of their approach.'

Prof Lord Broers,
former Vice-Chancellor of the University of Cambridge

'The Macat vision is exceptionally exciting. It focuses upon new modes of learning which analyse and explain seminal texts which have profoundly influenced world thinking and so social and economic development. It promotes the kind of critical thinking which is essential for any society and economy. This is the learning of the future.'

Rt Hon Charles Clarke, former UK Secretary of State for Education

'The Macat analyses provide immediate access to the critical conversation surrounding the books that have shaped their respective discipline, which will make them an invaluable resource to all of those, students and teachers, working in the field.'

Professor William Tronzo, University of California at San Diego

WAYS IN TO THE TEXT

KEY POINTS

- Hanna Batatu (1926–2000) was a Palestinian* political scientist and historian of the Middle East. He was educated at Harvard University and wrote extensive social histories of Iraq* and Syria.*

- *The Old Social Classes and the Revolutionary Movements of Iraq* describes the social, economic, and political factors that led to the Iraqi revolution of 1958.*

- *The Old Social Classes* uses unique historical sources to show how economic changes in Iraq produced a conflict between different social and economic classes.

Who Was Hanna Batatu?

Hanna Batatu was born in Jerusalem, Palestine, in 1926 and worked during his teenage years for the British Mandate* government. He left with his family for the United States after the 1948 Arab–Israeli war* that led to the establishment of the State of Israel.* In 1953, he graduated *summa cum laude* (with the highest grade possible) from Georgetown University's School of Foreign Service and then attended Harvard University, receiving a master's degree in Soviet* Studies. He planned to write a history of the Ba'th* and Communist* Parties of Iraq and Syria, arriving in Iraq in the late 1950s to start his research. His arrival coincided with the 1958 revolution* and this, in turn, encouraged him to focus his book solely on Iraq. He received his PhD from Harvard in June 1960 and continued to travel to Iraq over the decade from 1958 to 1968.[1]

Batatu worked at the American University of Beirut for 20 years from 1962. For most of that time, until a civil war began in 1975, Lebanon* was enjoying relative political calm and economic success. While he was there, Batatu completed his research and wrote his first book, *The Old Social Classes and the Revolutionary Movements of Iraq* published by Princeton University Press in 1978.

Lebanon's fortunes changed in the mid-1970s, when Palestinian forces, deprived of a base in Jordan* after the September 1970 civil war,* began to use Lebanon as a launching ground for attacks against Israel. When the Israelis invaded Lebanon in 1982, Batatu returned to the United States and Georgetown. He served as the Shaykh Sabah al-Salem al-Sabah Chair of Contemporary Arab Studies at Georgetown University from 1982 to 1994. From 1994 to 1999, Batatu continued to teach at Georgetown as Emeritus Professor and considered beginning a new research project on Palestine. By 1999, suffering from cancer, he moved back to Connecticut to live with his brother's family. Hanna Batatu died in the United States in 2000, aged 74.

What Does *The Old Social Classes* Say?

The Old Social Classes argues that a struggle between socio-economic classes* was the root cause of Iraq's 1958 revolution. During the late nineteenth and early twentieth centuries, Iraq had been integrated into the wider capitalist* world. The country joined the global capitalist economy because of technological innovations—such as railroads and steamships—and greater integration into the Ottoman* and later British economies. Economic change brought social change, Batatu writes, which transformed Iraq's "old social classes." These older social classes were based in part on material wealth, but also on other cultural and geographic factors, such as religion, tribal affiliation, and location in urban or rural areas. New socio-economic classes based on property ownership or financial income replaced these older social groupings over time. The struggle between remnants of older and emergent social classes defined the politics of the country in the period before and after World War II.* This struggle intensified after the war and ultimately led to the revolution of 1958.

The Old Social Classes is Batatu's history of economic integration, class formation, and revolution in Iraq. There are above all two things that make the text important. First, Batatu's work insisted that the category of social class was vital in analyzing and understanding Middle Eastern history. This approach was at odds with the claims of earlier writers that social class could not be used to describe or define Arab societies. These claims were based on the idea that the religion of Islam* (which many people saw as the main driving force behind Arab history) would keep people from becoming communists. Many people at the time Batatu was writing believed communism had no appeal for people in the Middle East. For example, George Kennan,* a prominent American diplomat and historian, once commented that "the fire of Moslem ideology" would hold the Soviet Union* at bay.[2] However, Batatu argues that economic forces and political ideas from across the world could indeed affect the Arab world.

The second important element of *The Old Social Classes* is the unprecedented amount of historical detail in the book, which runs to almost 1,300 pages. The text goes back in time to the nineteenth century when Iraq was under Ottoman rule and changes were already beginning to take place. It then moves on to the twentieth century when other forces—including communism, the movement towards Arab nationalism* and the Cold War* between the United States and the Soviet Union—all played a part in Iraq's class development.

Many other societies faced a similar story of global economic integration during the twentieth century. This did not, however, always happen in the same way in every place. Batatu's analysis delves deep into the Iraqi case and its special circumstances. In particular, he looks at the question of the political damage done to Iraq by its affiliation with British power after the invasion of 1914. Batatu argues that peaceful political evolution became impossible, not only because the majority of Iraqis saw British influence as illegitimate, but also because Britain so altered Iraq's social, political, and economic structure that conflict became inevitable.[3]

Batatu's book is still important for anyone wishing to understand Iraq—a country that has been unusually significant in world affairs for several decades. After the Americans invaded Iraq for the second time in 2003 (the first time was in 1991), Saqi Books republished *The Old Social Classes* the following year. This was no small commitment on the part of the publishers considering the book's length. They believed it would gain a new readership and new importance, given that there was such renewed interest in both the country and its history. This republication after more than twenty-five years is a testament to the book's remarkable staying power.

Why Does *The Old Social Classes* Matter?

The Old Social Classes remains one of the best social histories of any Middle Eastern country. For that reason alone, it is worth reading, despite what some would regard as its excessive length. It is also particularly relevant because of several ongoing conflicts in the Middle East. The outcome of the American invasion of Iraq in 2003, the subsequent civil war, and the rise of the so-called "Islamic State"* in 2014 can only be understood in terms of the local and regional history and politics that came before. In the past, as well as more recently, people have written books about the Middle East focusing on its problems from the point of view of international relations. Far fewer have written at the level of Batatu's work, which gives a deep and insightful analysis of *local* conditions.

The Old Social Classes is a challenging work because of its length. However, it gives readers a unique understanding of Iraqi history and the broad spectrum of Iraqis—from wealthy merchants to peasant farmers, from army officers to poverty-stricken intellectuals—who all helped to shape the country.

The Old Social Classes is important, too, because it runs counter to earlier trends in Middle Eastern history writing—trends that still re-emerge from time to time in contemporary academic or popular writing. First, Batatu's work extends back into the nineteenth century, a time when the Ottoman Empire governed Iraq. His description of the changes that were already taking place during this period counters the view usually found in writing about the Middle East. This is the idea that progress was *only* possible in the region after it fell under the influence of Western European empires in the early twentieth century.[4]

Batatu's work also helps to explain how both communism and Arab nationalism influenced Iraqi history. Batatu's account is complex and sensitive to the effects of these movements on different actors inside and outside Iraq, from the military to the working classes to foreign powers. His portrayal of communism and the part it played in Iraq in the years before the 1958 revolution is extensive. Batatu shows how Iraqis circulated communist ideas through local networks, how local conditions and concerns shaped the ideas themselves, and how the Iraqi Communist Party* used domestic economic and political issues to broaden their appeal to ordinary Iraqis.

NOTES

1   Bart Barnes, "Scholar Hanna Batatu, 74, Dies; Authority on Modern Iraq, Syria," *Washington Post*, June 28, 2000. See also E. Roger Owen, "The Historian as Witness: In Memory of Hanna Batatu (1926–2000)," *Harvard Middle Eastern and Islamic Review* 6 (2000–2001): 94–5.

2   Giles D. Harlow and George C. Maerz, eds., *Measures Short of War: The George F. Kennan Lectures at the National War College 1946–1947* (Washington, DC: National Defense University Press, 1991), 163.

3   Hanna Batatu, *The Old Social Classes and the Revolutionary Movements of Iraq: A Study of Iraq's Landed and Commercial Classes and of its Communists, Ba'thists and Free Officers* (Princeton, NJ: Princeton University Press, 1978), 63–152 and 224–318.

4   The problems of this approach are discussed most vividly in Edward Said, *Orientalism* (New York: Vintage Books, 1979), 255–60. For Iraq, there is the specific case of Stephen Hemsley Longrigg, *Four Centuries of Modern Iraq* (Oxford: Oxford University Press, 1925).

SECTION 1
INFLUENCES

MODULE 1
THE AUTHOR AND THE HISTORICAL CONTEXT

KEY POINTS

- *The Old Social Classes* remains one of the most detailed social histories of any Middle Eastern state in the twentieth century.

- Hanna Batatu's Palestinian* background fed his fascination with revolution. He was strongly influenced by works on the English Civil War* and the French and Russian Revolutions.*

- Batatu was particularly concerned with the political legitimacy of the modern Iraqi state and the pressures it was under as a result of decolonization* and Arab nationalism.*

Why Read This Text?

The Old Social Classes and the Revolutionary Movements of Iraq is one of the most important books on Iraq* and a vital piece of social history about a Middle Eastern country. The book's author, Hanna Batatu, was Palestinian by birth and spent most of his career teaching in Beirut, Lebanon.* Batatu's text uses a frame of analysis that was innovative for its time. This frame, socio-economic class* analysis, helped to revise the way scholars had previously interpreted change in Arab societies.

Batatu's book is part of a trend in historical analysis known as the "new social history,"* which examines the history of ordinary people, rather than that of the elite, for example kings and presidents. Batatu's book shows how ordinary laborers, army personnel, and local intellectuals brought about a revolution in the politics of their country.

> 66 When I began working on *The Old Social Classes* in the late 1950s, I was irresistibly drawn to the literature on revolution. I do not know precisely why, but probably my Palestinian background explains it. The disruptions of the lives and world of many Palestinians made them, so to speak, natural rebels. 99
>
> Hanna Batatu, "The Old Social Classes Revisited"

The Old Social Classes is important, too, because of its detail and sources. At nearly 1,300 pages long, the text includes an immense amount of information about Iraqi society. For this reason, it is almost seen as an encyclopedia for historians of Iraq and it continues to help scholars working on Iraqi history contextualize their research questions. In writing his book, Batatu also gained access to sensitive police surveillance files for the period after World War II* and to political prisoners held in Iraqi prisons. These unique sources were of great value to his analysis. The oral histories he gathered are invaluable in interpreting key moments in Iraqi history.

Author's Life

Born in Jerusalem in 1926, Hanna Batatu worked for the British Mandate government* of Palestine in its postal service when he was a teenager. After the 1948 Arab–Israeli war* and the subsequent establishment of the State of Israel,* Batatu migrated with his family to the United States. He settled in Stamford, Connecticut and worked for a time for a carpet company before going to university. In 1953, he graduated *summa cum laude* (with the highest grade possible) from Georgetown University's School of Foreign Service, then went to Harvard University for his master's degree in Soviet* Studies. While at Harvard, he planned to write a history of Communist* Parties in the Middle East, but then decided to focus on the Ba'th* and

Communist Parties of Iraq and Syria.* He began work in the late 1950s, arriving in Iraq for his field research in time to witness the revolution in 1958. The experience encouraged him to devote his first book solely to Iraq. During his time there, Batatu accessed secret police records as a result of his friendships and connections at Harvard. He was awarded his PhD from Harvard in June 1960, but travelled to Iraq several times over the decade from 1958 to 1968.[1] Princeton University Press first published *The Old Social Classes* in 1978.

Batatu joined the faculty of the American University of Beirut in Lebanon* in 1962 and worked there for 20 years. After Israel invaded Lebanon in 1982, Batatu returned to the United States and worked for the rest of his career at Georgetown University. He was the Shaykh Sabah al-Salem al-Sabah Chair of Contemporary Arab Studies from 1982 to 1994. He died at the age of 74 on June 24, 2000, in Winsted, Connecticut.

Author's Background

Batatu wrote *The Old Social Classes* during a period marked by two important global historical events. The first event was decolonization, the overturning of colonial control in a state that was dependent on an outside power. In the case of the Middle East, this took place at around the same time as the rise and fall of Arab nationalist ideology. Arab nationalism was the idea that all Arabic-speaking peoples belong to one nation. The second event was the intensification of the Cold War* between the two nuclear-armed superpowers,* the United States and the Soviet Union.* These issues provided the political and intellectual backdrop to Batatu's work.

These two areas of conflict—between the United States and the Soviet Union over power in the Middle East, and between a number of Arab states over the meaning of "Arab nationhood"—generated several crises of legitimacy (lawful validity) for Middle Eastern regimes. The way borders were drawn in the twentieth-century Middle East was a key part of these crises.

Before World War I,* most of the region was part of a single entity, the Ottoman Empire.* The Ottoman Empire entered the war on the side of the Central Powers (alongside Germany, Austria-Hungary, and Bulgaria) but this alliance was defeated by Western European powers, together with the United States. At the 1919 Paris Peace Conference* following the war, the Allied Powers (America, Britain, France, and Italy) created several new, supposedly independent Arab-majority states. These states—Palestine, Transjordan,* Syria and Lebanon, and Iraq—were called "mandates." Under the mandate system, a larger, more powerful country was given control over the affairs of the new state under the supervision of a new international organization, the League of Nations. The more powerful country was to guide the new state toward complete independence. In the Middle East, Britain was given mandates over Palestine, Transjordan, and Iraq, while France gained a mandate over Syria and Lebanon.

As the European empires weakened after World War II, the Arab states gained increasing control over their own affairs. Egypt, which was never under mandate control, had been nominally independent since 1922 and gained full independence from Britain in 1952 following the Egyptian revolution.* This revolution brought a new president to power, Gamal Abdel Nasser.* Nasser argued for the political unification of the Arabic-speaking world and was the most prominent challenger to the state system imposed by European powers. The Egyptian president saw the existing borders as false, foreign impositions on what should rightfully be a single Arab nation.

Batatu's work is concerned with the legitimacy of an Iraqi state within this Middle Eastern state system—a system that was under attack at that time by a hugely popular Arab leader. He saw Iraq as having been so damaged by its affiliation with British power that peaceful political evolution there was impossible.

NOTES

1   Bart Barnes, "Scholar Hanna Batatu, 74, Dies; Authority on Modern Iraq,
     Syria," *Washington Post*, June 28, 2000. See also E. Roger Owen, "The
     Historian as Witness: In Memory of Hanna Batatu (1926–2000)," *Harvard
     Middle Eastern and Islamic Review* 6 (2000–2001): 94–5.

ACADEMIC CONTEXT

KEY POINTS

- *The Old Social Classes* is a historical study concerned with discovering the long-term causes of the Iraqi revolution of 1958.*

- Hanna Batatu's book was part of a new trend in historical studies known as "new social history,"* which brought ordinary social, political, and economic groups into historical accounts.

- For Batatu, what primarily divided people in society was the issue of ownership of property. Those who owned property obtained economic and political power over those who did not.

The Work in its Context

Hanna Batatu's history of class relations in Iraqi society, *The Old Social Classes and the Revolutionary Movements of Iraq*, was part of an overall shift in historical analysis in the 1950s and 1960s. This was a period dominated by the ideological battles between capitalism* and communism* that characterized the Cold War.* Looking for a different viewpoint, contemporary historians began to move away from state-centered political history and the actions of the political elite. The new social history focused instead on "the processes affecting the great majority of people alive," such as family structures, urban life, race, and social mobility.[1]

This new social history movement covered areas like labor, women and gender, family, class, and education. The book that first heralded this new approach in history was E. P. Thompson's* *The Making of the English Working Class*, published in 1963. Thompson wrote that his

> ❝ I think we may accept that the twenty years following the Second World War saw a sharp decline in political and religious history, in the use of 'ideas' as an explanation of history, and a remarkable turn to socio-economic history and to historical explanation in terms of 'social forces'. ❞
>
> Eric Hobsbawm, "The Revival of Narrative: Some Comments"

main quarrel was with historical narratives that "obscure the agency of working people, the degree to which they contributed by conscious efforts, to the making of history."[2] New social history, which reached its peak in the 1970s, had several aims. These included bringing varied social, political, and economic groups into the study of history, a move away from "top-down" explanations of social phenomena by focusing on the elite and the powerful, and a concern for the political empowerment of groups that had previously been ignored by historians and social scientists. Batatu's focus on ordinary Iraqis and their struggles reflected the concerns of many social historians at this time to tell a story from "the bottom up."[3]

Overview of the Field
The new social history was a varied field, but one of its major streams of thinking was Marxist.* This means it related to the theories and ideas of Karl Marx,* a nineteenth-century German philosopher and socialist,* who wrote several important books including *The Communist Manifesto* and *Das Kapital*.[4]

In his writings, Marx put forward a theory of historical development that emphasized material conditions, such as technological capacity or production levels. The material conditions of life, he argued, are produced through human labor, and within any given society there would be a division of labor between an upper class who owned the means of production and a lower class who worked in them. These classes, Marx said, would inevitably come into conflict. To him, history was the story of the lower classes overthrowing the upper class and producing a new social order. According to Marx, history is meant "to distinguish between the material transformation of the economic conditions of production … and the legal, political, religious, artistic or philosophic … forms in which men become conscious of this conflict and fight it out."[5]

In other words, legal history, religious history, and intellectual history are all subordinate—or secondary—to the history of "material transformation." Marx argues that the "structure" that underpins society is based fundamentally on the production and acquisition of property and material goods. So within this new social history, scholars such as E. P. Thompson and Eric Hobsbawm* used Marx's ideas about the upper and lower classes to increase the number of actors on the historical stage. Critically, however, they tried to do so without reducing individuals simply to a "class." So, for instance, E. P. Thompson said, "I am seeking to rescue the poor stockinger, the Luddite* cropper, the 'obsolete' hand-loom weaver, the 'utopian' artisan … from the enormous condescension of posterity."[6] To these new social historians, it was important not only to understand the power of Marx's "material transformation," but also to recognize the individuals in the lower classes, who, as Thompson argues, were involved in the "making of history." Batatu's work is part of this overall trend, explaining the development of broad-based social classes in Iraq* and the movements that sprang from them, based on a shared background.

Academic Influences

Batatu directly acknowledged his debt to Marx and his ideas about material conditions and class. Additionally, when he was writing *The Old Social Classes* he was also influenced by two other important thinkers, Max Weber* and, interestingly enough, by the writings of the nineteenth-century President of the United States James Madison.* Batatu mentions both men in the first chapter of his book: "To be more explicit, I find it difficult not to agree with James Madison, Karl Marx, and Max Weber that 'property' and 'lack of property' form the fundamental elements of the class … situation, and that this antithesis contains the seeds of an antagonistic relationship."[7] For Batatu, the ownership of property was the main factor dividing individuals in society—a factor that led to a wide gap in economic fortunes and then a struggle for political power.

Batatu's theories about historical progress are similar to those of Marx and other social historians writing at the time, but he commented after the book's publication, "I did not accept all of Marx's concepts and those I accepted I did not accept uncritically. Nor did I use them in an *a priori* or mechanical fashion."[8] As evidence, Batatu mentioned his other intellectual debt—to British empiricism,* "especially its scrupulous regard for facts and its distrust of large generalizations."[9] British empiricism emerged in the late seventeenth century, primarily in the writings of philosopher John Locke,* who believed that human knowledge is based upon experience. In *The Old Social Classes*, Locke's doctrine appears in the form of Batatu's huge accumulation of data—the text is nearly 1,300 pages long—and his lack of theoretical argument. Indeed, aside from a few comments at the beginning, *The Old Social Classes* does not spend a lot of effort on arguing theory.

NOTES

1 Laurence Vesey, "The 'New' Social History in the Context of American Historical Writing," *Reviews in American History* 7 (1979), 4.

2 E. P. Thompson, *The Making of the English Working Class* (London: Victor Gollancz, 1980), 11.

3 Paul E. Johnson, "Looking Back at Social History," *Reviews in American History* 39 (2011): 380.

4   Karl Marx and Frederick Engels, *Manifesto of the Communist Party*, trans. Samuel Moore, (London: William Reeves, 1888); Karl Marx, *Capital*, ed. Frederick Engels (London: Swan Sonnenschein, Lowry & Co., 1887).

5   Karl Marx, *A Contribution to the Critique of Political Economy* (Moscow: Progress Publishers, 1977), 2.

6   Thompson, *The Making of the English Working Class*, 11.

7   Hanna Batatu, *The Old Social Classes and the Revolutionary Movements of Iraq: A Study of Iraq's Landed and Commercial Classes and of its Communists, Ba'thists and Free Officers* (Princeton, NJ: Princeton University Press, 1978), 7.

8   Hanna Batatu, "The Old Social Classes Revisited," in *The Iraqi Revolution of 1958: The Old Social Classes Revisited*, ed. Robert A. Fernea and W. Roger Louis (London: I.B. Tauris, 1991), 212.

9   Batatu, "The Old Social Classes Revisited," 212.

MODULE 3
THE PROBLEM

KEY POINTS

- A major question for historians of the Middle East at this time was whether socio-economic class* could even be used in analyzing Middle Eastern societies.

- Some scholars argued that Middle Eastern societies had no "class consciousness," perhaps as a result of the influence of Islam,* or that communist* ideals appealed only to a minority of people.

- Hanna Batatu claimed that political and social conflict in Iraq* arose as a result of the formation of socio-economic classes.

Core Question

The core question at the heart of Hanna Batatu's *The Old Social Classes and the Revolutionary Movements of Iraq* is: what were the social origins and outcomes of the Iraqi revolution of July 1958?* To answer that question, Batatu uses sociological class analysis. His aim was to trace how Iraq's "old social classes" were transformed as the country integrated into the global capitalist* economic system. According to Batatu, these new class formations were motivated by communist ideology, and the subsequent class struggle resulted in the Iraqi revolution of 1958.

At this time, new social history* methods such as sociological class analysis were seen as not relevant to the Middle East. Socio-economic classes were regarded as typical of advanced, industrial nations, whereas Middle Eastern societies were thought to have radically different social structures dominated by other concerns, usually religious. Take, for

> ❝ It has often been maintained that the classic sociological class analysis ... is inapplicable to Arab societies, or that in Arab societies there are no such things as 'classes.' This is a generalization apart from the evidence, at least as far as post-World War I* Arab societies are concerned. ❞
>
> Hanna Batatu, *The Old Social Classes*

instance, Palestinian* American Edward Said's* critique of H. A. R. Gibb,* Batatu's supervisor at Harvard University: "The heart of Gibb's argument is that Islam ... has an ultimate precedence and domination over all life in the Islamic Orient."[1] From this viewpoint, there is little room for analysis of anything that would oppose Islam, such as a system of communism that denies the very existence of God. Batatu was asking a question that previous texts on Iraq, confining themselves primarily to issues seen during the British Mandate,* had not sought to answer.[2] Most research into communism in the Middle East at this time suggested that it was an idea that had simply been implanted by foreign influences.

The Participants

Several post-1945 thinkers argued that the analysis of social class was not relevant when examining social and political dynamics in Middle Eastern societies. Scholars such as Walter Laqueur* viewed communist parties in the Middle East as foreign implants, appealing only to the urban educated and cultured, rather than social movements with broad popularity.[3] Others thought Arab societies were tribally based systems embedded in an unchanging Islam. In fact, Islam was sometimes seen at this time as "a bulwark"—or barrier—against atheistic* communism.[4] Communist politics, it was argued, depended on society dividing according to socio-cultural background, so the formation of a "proletariat"—"working class"—was "not rooted in the homegrown social structure of Middle Eastern countries."[5] As a result, little importance was given to communist assessments of economic and social ills in the politics of Middle Eastern countries.

Batatu also departed from another widely accepted theory about Middle Eastern history. "The decline thesis" was based on the historical tradition of defining the rise and fall of civilizations. H. A. R. Gibb and Harold Bowen* were the best-known supporters of this theory as it applied to the Middle East. They argued that Islamic civilization had reached its peak during the early medieval period,* roughly the ninth to the eleventh centuries, and then experienced a period of continual decline.[6] This view not only ruled out change and renewal, but it also compared the Middle East unfavorably with Europe. Middle Eastern societies were seen as static, decadent, and degenerating, while European historical change was natural, progressive, and authoritative.[7]

The Contemporary Debate

New social historians of the Middle East during the 1960s and 1970s challenged the status quo on class analysis and "the decline thesis." There were two major trends in historical thinking that broke away from these earlier approaches to Middle Eastern history.

The first trend supported class-based analysis. Along with Ervand Abrahamian,* who published his *Iran between Two Revolutions* in 1982,[8] Batatu tackled the question of revolution with an extremely detailed, practical approach. *The Old Social Classes* is an impressively thorough book and even Batatu said that the "large amount of facts that I collected … had a paralysing effect on me."[9] This "paralysis" led Batatu to limit his arguments carefully—the data suggested multiple possible interpretations. However, when he answered his core question, it meant his arguments were well supported by this vast collection of data. Batatu's description of Iraq's active Communist Party* disproved claims that communism could not work in the Middle East without Soviet* assistance.[10] He amassed significant evidence of the appeal of local Iraqi communist organizations and highlighted their weak ties to the Soviet Union. Batatu's work was highly regarded by Middle Eastern scholars, both at the time and since, for its explanation both of how classes formed and the appeal of communist ideas in Iraqi society.

Batatu addressed a second conservative trend, that of modernization theory.* Modernization theory assumes the superiority of social, political, and economic development in Western European societies. It argues that all societies can, through economic development, reach levels of development and democracy* that "resemble Europe."[11] Modernization theory provided a way to move on from the "decline thesis," offering a plan for the proper development of "backward" regions. At the heart of this theory was the idea that European models could be exported to remake other parts of the world.[12]

The Old Social Classes was published at roughly the same time as an influential work of modernization theory, Bernard Lewis's* *The Emergence of Modern Turkey*.[13] Lewis looks for the elements of traditional Turkish society that contributed to or hindered the country's progress toward a modern capitalist democracy. In contrast, Batatu's text rejects modernization theory. Batatu points out the inequality, violence, and injustice that came with the imposition of capitalism and imperialism* in Iraq during the British Mandate period. According to Batatu, modernization actually led less toward a democratic utopia—a place where everything is perfect—and more toward class struggle and revolution.

NOTES

1   Edward Said, *Orientalism* (New York: Vintage Books, 1979), 278.

2   There were very few studies of Iraq available during the 1960s and 1970s. One of note is Peter Sluglett, *Britain in Iraq, 1914–1932* (London: Ithaca Press, 1976).

3   Walter Laqueur, *Communism and Nationalism in the Middle East* (New York: Praeger, 1956), 273–4.

4   US Secretary of State George Kennan most famously pronounced this idea in a speech in 1947 at the National War College. See Matthew F. Jacobs, *Imagining the Middle East: The Building of an American Foreign Policy, 1918–1967* (Chapel Hill, NC: UNC Press, 2011), 78–9.

5   Joel Beinin, "Class and Politics in Middle Eastern Societies. A Review Article," *Comparative Studies in Society and History* 28, no. 3 (1986): 552.

6   H. A. R. Gibb and Harold Bowen, *Islamic Society and the West: A Study of the Impact of Western Civilization on Moslem Culture in the Near East* (London: Oxford University Press, 1950).

7   Huri İslamoğlu and Çağlar Keyder, "Agenda for Ottoman History," *The Ottoman Empire and the World-Economy*, ed. Huri İslamoğlu-İnan (Cambridge: Cambridge University Press, 1987), 44–6.

8   Ervand Abrahamian, *Iran between Two Revolutions* (Princeton, NJ: Princeton University Press, 1982).

9   Hanna Batatu, "The Old Social Classes Revisited," in *The Iraqi Revolution of 1958: The Old Social Classes Revisited*, ed. Robert A. Fernea and W. Roger Louis (London: I.B. Tauris, 1991), 213.

10 Beinin, "Class and Politics," 552.

11 Seymour Martin Lipset, "Some Social Requisites of Democracy: Economic Development and Political Legitimacy," *The American Political Science Review* 53 (1959): 101.

12 Daniel Lerner, *The Passing of Traditional Society: Modernizing the Middle East* (New York: The Free Press, 1958), 47.

13 Bernard Lewis, *The Emergence of Modern Turkey* (London: Oxford University Press, 1968).

THE AUTHOR'S CONTRIBUTION

KEY POINTS

- Hanna Batatu argues that when Iraq* joined the global capitalist* system at the end of the nineteenth and the start of the twentieth centuries older social groupings based on tribal, ethnic, or religious ties became less important, while new socio-economic classes,* characterized by control over property or production, came to the fore.

- *The Old Social Classes* refutes the idea that class was not an appropriate way to analyze Middle Eastern societies.

- Other works at this time offered similar assessments, but none on the scale of Batatu's analysis of Iraqi history.

Author's Aims

In *The Old Social Classes and the Revolutionary Movements of Iraq*, Hanna Batatu states that his aim is to "find out whether a class approach would open to view historical relations or social features that would otherwise remain beyond vision."[1] In the second and third sections of his book, Batatu discusses three movements in particular. These are as follows:

- The communist* movement. Those whose ideologies derive from the writings of Karl Marx* and are in favor of the collective ownership of property and social revolution to produce a classless society.
- The Ba'thist* movement. Those who favored the concept of the rebirth of the Arab nation through economic, social, and political progress.

❝ Inevitably, the relations between Iraqis became less and less governed by kinship or religious standing or considerations of birth, and more and more by material possessions. Property also assumed a greater significance as a basis of social stratification and in the scale of power. ❞

Hanna Batatu, *The Old Social Classes*

- The Free Officers Movement.* Those who were part of a secretive group of Iraqi military officers who also believed in the notion of all Arabs being part of one state, but who wanted to bring it about by deposing what they saw as a corrupt regime.

Batatu wanted to "trace the origins of these movements, seek out the roots of the thoughts and emotions by which they are impelled, describe their organizational forms and social structures, reconstruct their internal life … and assess the impact they had on their country and its history."[2] For the most part, Batatu is successful in explaining historical change in both Iraqi class relations and the three political movements he analyzed.

Batatu wanted to go further than these initial concerns, though, and bring about a real change in the study of Middle Eastern societies. By putting class at the forefront of his work, he demolishes the concept of "Arab exceptionalism,*" which held that "in Arab societies there are no such things as 'classes'."[3] According to the idea of Arab exceptionalism,[4] Arab societies were impervious to global political trends, such as the formation of socio–economic classes, because of unique historical experiences, often traced to Islam.* For Batatu, this idea was a matter of ideology rather than something that could be supported by scholarship.

The theory of "Arab exceptionalism" also needlessly complicated an analysis of communist parties in the region. Since Arab societies were impervious to the kinds of changes happening in the rest of the world, the argument ran that communism could only be instigated, imported from, and nurtured by an external power—in this case, the Soviet Union.* Such a view of Arab societies therefore supported the idea that outside intervention* was justified to "defend" a nation against external communist influence. The broader international implications of the idea of Arab exceptionalism may be seen most dramatically in the Eisenhower Doctrine.* American President Dwight D. Eisenhower* laid out this American foreign-policy doctrine in January 1957 in a message to US Congress.* Eisenhower said the United States would "defend the territorial integrity and the political independence of any nation in the area against Communist armed aggression."[5] The Eisenhower Doctrine justified sending American troops to Lebanon* the following year. Batatu wanted to overturn the whole idea of "Arab exceptionalism," by giving an account of Arab communism that clearly showed its local roots. According to Batatu, the communist ideas circulating in Iraq were not a result of "Communist armed aggression" as Eisenhower asserted, but a result of the dramatic economic and social changes occurring within Iraq. Batatu's description of the Iraqi Communist Party* reveals both its origins in that process of change and its limited links with the government of the Soviet Union.

Approach

While it clearly touches on theories from both Karl Marx and Max Weber,* *The Old Social Classes* is not a book weighed down with theories. To prove that class is an important analytical lens through which to view Arab societies, Batatu prefers to provide overwhelming evidence rather than extensive theoretical arguments. In this way, he avoids a dogmatic reiteration of established theory. Batatu notes that it is not necessary "to accept the different series of concepts" that Marx and Weber use with respect to class, "or their underlying assumptions or implications unless, of course, they are empirically* verifiable or applicable to the case in hand."[6]

As a result, several sections of the book are burdened by the vast scope of Batatu's collected data, with pages at a time devoted to charts and tables. For instance, in just one chapter eight pages are occupied by a chart and diagram detailing the biographical details of the leaders of Iraq's various communist organizations.[7] While this wealth of information is useful in supporting Batatu's claims, it also results in a narrative driven by detail rather than argument. Moreover, some of the details are difficult for historians to verify and corroborate. In the latter part of his book, Batatu included a number of interviews with Iraqi statesmen. These interviews, with such prominent individuals as foreign minister Hashim Jawad* and former president Abd ar-Rahman Arif,*[8] are important for the story. However, a reader must approach oral histories carefully, as the historian himself becomes part of the production of knowledge (since he or she becomes both interviewer and interpreter).

Contribution in Context

The underlying argument at work in *The Old Social Classes* is that Iraqi history is best understood through a class-based historical analysis. Batatu claims that over time, the country developed socio-economic classes and the struggle between these classes defined the politics of the country, particularly after World War II.* Batatu wrote his history during the Cold War,* a period when the United States and Soviet Union were competing for influence in the Middle East and elsewhere around the world. This competition involved interpretations of history, capitalism, and communism that relate to the claims in Batatu's text. Batatu is not shy about his chosen analytical frame. At the very start of the book, he clearly declares his interest in Marxist* theory and believes it can reveal something new about Iraqi history.[9]

Still, it would be a mistake to think of Batatu's text as simply a partisan intervention to support one superpower* or another. He is clearly most interested in the fortunes of the Iraqi people and the local outcomes of struggles for political power. One observer notes that Batatu wrote "for truth and in the interests of doing proper justice to the lives of those who had struggled, and often died, for large causes."[10] Moreover, even considering Batatu's beliefs, his approach to a material, structural analysis in his work of social history is significant. While earlier histories of Iraq focused on the country's political leaders and elder statesmen, Batatu investigates other individuals and groups and shows their influence on events.[11] Because he compiles so much evidence, his conclusions are very well documented, particularly in the first two parts of the text. While Batatu may be criticized for seeing much of Iraq's history through the lens of class, his vast array of data means he cannot be overlooked in any serious consideration of Iraqi history. In addition, Batatu must be given credit for noting the potential importance of factors outside the frame of a Marxist history. For instance, while he believes economic conditions were mainly responsible for the 1920 Iraqi revolt,* he adds that he does not wish to "deny the role of contingent personal factors or of moral influences."[12] While *The Old Social Classes* sees material economic conditions as the driver of historical change, it is not totally rigid in its interpretations.

NOTES

1   Hanna Batatu, *The Old Social Classes and the Revolutionary Movements of Iraq: A Study of Iraq's Landed and Commercial Classes and of its Communists, Ba'thists and Free Officers* (Princeton, NJ: Princeton University Press, 1978), xxi.

2   Batatu, *Old Social Classes*, xxi.

3   Batatu, *Old Social Classes*, 5.

4   For more on "Arab exceptionalism," see Alfred Stepan and Graeme B.
     Robertson, "An 'Arab' More than 'Muslim' Electoral Gap," *Journal of
     Democracy* 14 (2003), 30–44; John Waterbury, "Democracy without
     Democrats?" in *Democracy without Democrats? The Renewal of Politics in
     the Muslim World*, ed. Ghassan Salamé (London: I.B. Tauris, 1994), 23–47.

5   Dwight D. Eisenhower, "Special Message to the Congress on the Situation
     in the Middle East," January 5, 1957, online by Gerhard Peters and John
     T. Woolley, *The American Presidency Project*, accessed February 23, 2015,
     www.presidency.ucsb.edu/ws/?pid=11007.

6   Batatu, *Old Social Classes*, 7.

7   Batatu, *Old Social Classes*, 414–21.

8   Batatu, *Old Social Classes*, 836, 1062, 1073–4.

9   Batatu, *Old Social Classes*, 5.

10 E. Roger Owen, "The Historian as Witness: In Memory of Hanna Batatu
     (1926–2000)," *Harvard Middle Eastern and Islamic Review* 6 (2000–2001),
     107.

11 These most prominently include Majid Khadduri's books on Iraq,
     Independent Iraq: A Study in Iraqi Politics Since 1932 (London: Oxford
     University Press, 1951); *Republican Iraq: A Study in Iraqi Politics Since the
     Revolution of 1958* (London: Oxford University Press, 1969); and *Socialist
     Iraq: A Study in Iraqi Politics Since 1968* (Washington, DC: Middle East
     Institute, 1978).

12 Batatu, *Old Social Classes*, 174–5.

SECTION 2
IDEAS

MODULE 5
MAIN IDEAS

KEY POINTS

- Hanna Batatu's *The Old Social Classes* revolves around three major historical themes: the economic transformation of Iraq's* older social groupings into socio-economic classes;* the rise of communist* organizations and dissemination of communist ideas; and the specific political changes and events in Iraq during the 1950s that produced a revolution.*

- Batatu's central argument is that, after Iraq joined the global economy of the twentieth century, socio-economic classes formed, defined by ownership of property and production, and came into conflict, resulting in the revolution of 1958.

- Batatu set himself the task of meticulously detailing the economic and intellectual changes in Iraqi society, producing a highly detailed study of over 1,000 pages.

Key Themes

The main themes of Hanna Batatu's *The Old Social Classes and the Revolutionary Movements of Iraq* are the three factors that he believed led to Iraq's revolution in July 1958:

- The material basis of class.
- The ideological basis of communism.
- The historical basis on which different political and social trends came into conflict.

Firstly, Batatu examines the material formation of social class. He argues two main points here. First, that the gradual integration of Iraq

> ❝ Since the existing distribution of the goods and powers of life did not favor the bulk of the people ... and since no change compatible with current and incessantly mounting desires could be brought about by legal action ... the underground—the by now natural habitat of Iraqi Communists—came into its own. ❞
>
> Hanna Batatu, *The Old Social Classes*

into the global capitalist* system over the late nineteenth and early twentieth centuries had a profound impact on certain groups within Iraqi society. Second, that the British invasion and occupation of Iraq after World War I* significantly altered the way these changes happened. This is because British officials created a new Iraqi government, installed a foreign king, and produced a new political class that used its power to enrich itself.

Examining the ideological basis of communism, Batatu reveals how Iraqi communism was a specifically Iraqi institution. Iraq's communist groups, though aware of European ideas, actually grew out of several intellectual streams in Middle Eastern thought.

Finally, Batatu tackles the political and social events leading up to the revolution and in its aftermath. His main idea here is to show how various political movements came together and interacted during the revolutionary period. Batatu argues that a series of important uprisings created common ground among the Arab nationalist,* communist and Ba'thist* groups that were all present in Iraq at the time. The Baghdad Pact* of 1955, an anti-Soviet* security agreement and military alliance sponsored by Great Britain and the United States and including Iran and Iraq among others, united all these groups in opposition. This common ground made a popular revolution possible and that revolution had significant consequences for both Iraq and the Middle East in general.

Exploring the Ideas

Batatu describes the turmoil of Iraqi society in the nineteenth and twentieth centuries as "old ties, loyalties, and concepts were undermined, eroded, or swept away" by Iraq's "tying up ... to a world market anchored on big industry."[1] Beginning in the nineteenth century, his analysis pays particular attention to changes in Iraq's countryside and "the diversity of Iraqis."[2] Following "the development of towns, of the central government, of commerce and of communications," Batatu believes that the basis of people's lives changed. Material wealth, such as the ownership of land, provided new political opportunities to those groups associated with European powers.[3]

The British invasion of Iraq began at the end of 1914, leading to the fall of Baghdad in 1917 and the subsequent occupation of the country. To maintain their rule, the British gave landowners and other private capitalists legal powers over peasants and workers.[4] Batatu argues that "this new economic power of the shaikhs and aghas [the landowning tribal leaders] was, however, in its essence a concealed threat ... alienating them from the only real source of their power: their tribe."[5] As this tribal power declined and the gaps in society widened, new social forces came into play. Eventually, the ruling class suffered from an "inherent inability ... to cope effectively with serious social unbalances," which involved "marked expansion in the size of the educated middle class and its limited economic and political opportunities, [and] the rise in the consciousness and desires of the peasantry and town workers."[6]

This rise in social consciousness came about as a result of communist ideas. The prominent Islamic* revivalist Abd ar-Rahman al-Kawakibi* was a major figure in the emergence of communism in Iraq. Al-Kawakibi argued for what Batatu called "an egalitarian interpretation of Islam," which bore a striking resemblance to the rhetoric of communism.[7] According to Batatu, the Iraqi Communist

Party* was an amalgam of ideas that shared its roots with Arab socialism,* nationalism* and feminism.[8]

Batatu argues that a number of events in the period following World War II,* the formation of new social classes, and communist ideology all came together to produce a revolution. The 1940s saw major political upheavals in the Middle East, including a war in 1948 in Palestine,* the 1952 Egyptian Revolution,* and the 1956 Suez Crisis* when Israel,* France, and Britain invaded Egypt. The most significant event in Iraq during this period was the 1948 uprising known as "al-Wathbah," or "The Leap." Massive demonstrations against the extension of treaty relations with Great Britain resulted in repression, bloodshed, and martial law.* Batatu describes it as "the social subsoil of Baghdad in revolt against hunger and unequal burdens."[9] Demonstrations of popular discontent like al-Wathbah were not immediately successful in overturning the regime, but Batatu notes that "the basic conditions of existence that had made for communism … would in the next decade evoke and reevoke forces which it would not be within the powers of the police to lay."[10] Politics both inside and outside Iraq would diminish the ability of the state to suppress discontent. The revolution was not accomplished in one night, but involved both long-term factors and shorter-term political affairs.

Language and Expression

Batatu's text was aimed at an academic audience, but he also dedicated his work "To the People of Iraq." While pages and pages are devoted to tables and charts, observers at the time stated, "The Iraqi people … have found a worthy chronicler of their recent past."[11] This tension between academic rigor and an intended popular audience defines the language and expression in this large book. In early parts of the text, the language is highly academic and complex—including one sentence of 111 words. Later, particularly in the sections detailing the al–Wathbah insurrection and the revolution itself, the text is vigorous and engaging.[12]

This tension has affected the way the book has been received. Batatu's second chapter, "Of the Diversity of Iraqis, the Incohesiveness of Their Society, and Their Progress in the Monarchic Period toward a Consolidated Political Structure," contains some of his clearest writing and argument. This chapter was included in a work edited by prominent scholars of the Middle East, Albert Hourani*, Philip Khoury,* and Mary C. Wilson.*[13] Other sections of the book are made up of facts and tables, which led one critic to complain: "It will never stand accused of tightly-knit argumentation or compact, rigorous analysis."[14] The combination of encyclopedic documentation and gripping narrative is highly informative, but *The Old Social Classes* is a complex read and this has limited its reach.

NOTES

1   Hanna Batatu, *The Old Social Classes and the Revolutionary Movements of Iraq: A Study of Iraq's Landed and Commercial Classes and of its Communists, Ba'thists and Free Officers* (Princeton, NJ: Princeton University Press, 1978), 1113.

2   The quote comes from one of Batatu's chapter headings. See Batatu, *Old Social Classes,* 13–36.

3   Batatu, *Old Social Classes*, 78.

4   Batatu, *Old Social Classes*, 89–93.

5   Batatu, *Old Social Classes*, 78.

6   Batatu, *Old Social Classes*, 351.

7   Batatu, *Old Social Classes*, 367–70.

8   Batatu, *Old Social Classes*, 389–403.

9   Batatu, *Old Social Classes,* 545.

10 Batatu, *Old Social Classes*, 571.

11 Marion Farouk-Sluglett and Peter Sluglett, review of "Book II: The Communists and Their Movement," in *The Old Social Classes and the Revolutionary Movements of Iraq: A Study of Iraq's Landed and Commercial Classes and of its Communists, Ba'thists and Free Officers,* by Hanna Batatu, *MERIP Reports* 97 (1981): 27.

12 Batatu, *The Old Social Classes*, 545–66 and 764–807.

13 Albert Hourani, Philip Khoury, and Mary C. Wilson, eds., *The Modern Middle East: A Reader* (London: I.B. Tauris, 2005), 503–28.

14 James A. Bill, review of *The Old Social Classes and the Revolutionary Movements of Iraq: A Study of Iraq's Old Landed and Commercial Classes and of its Communists, Ba'thists and Free Officers*, by Hanna Batatu, *American Political Science Review* 74 (1980): 530.

MODULE 6
SECONDARY IDEAS

KEY POINTS

- Hanna Batatu's secondary ideas involve the considerable changes that took place during the late Ottoman* period in Iraq;* the relationship of tribal alliances and rural groups with Iraq's major cities; and the specific Iraqi experience of European economic and political imperialism.*

- These subsidiary ideas challenge previous scholars' claims that Iraq under Ottoman rule was stagnant, and suggest a different interpretation of the urban–rural divide in Iraq.

- The idea of a vibrant Ottoman Iraq reflected changing views about the Ottoman Empire generally. Batatu argues that the Ottoman Emipre was not in decline, but was vigorously reconstructing, a process cut short by World War I.*

Other Ideas

Underlying Hanna Batatu's major themes in *The Old Social Classes and the Revolutionary Movements of Iraq* is an examination of other social and political factors in Iraq during the nineteenth and twentieth centuries. Batatu offers a detailed description of Iraq under Ottoman rule in the century before World War I. When *The Old Social Classes* was published, one of the controversies it raised concerned the nature and vigor of social change during the Ottoman period. Earlier works had suggested that in nineteenth-century Iraq, its "civilization, politics, arms were universal and static."[1] Even studies of the country that examined social change tended to focus on politics at the elite level.[2]

> ❝ In some of its aspects, at least in terms of its social origins, Iraq's revolution was a rural revolution, or a revolution of the small country towns and of partially urbanized forces of rural origin against Iraq's chief city and its governing class. ❞
>
> Hanna Batatu, *The Egyptian, Syrian and Iraqi Revolutions*

Batatu also sought to explain tribal politics and the relationship of the countryside to the cities. In 1966, renowned Middle East historian Albert Hourani* gave a paper entitled "Ottoman Reform and the Politics of the Notables,"[3] which built on German social theorist Max Weber's* idea of the "patriciate." Weber divided cities according to whether they were ruled by patricians (noblemen or aristocrats), a single sovereign (prince or king), or plebes (the peasantry).[4] In Hourani's "politics of the notables," a small urban aristocratic class dominated Ottoman provinces during the nineteenth century. Batatu, on the other hand, highlighted the importance of Iraqi tribes and how their particular alliances influenced urban politics during the period.

Batatu's text is significant at the level of global history, too, particularly with regard to the impact of the Industrial Revolution* and the expansion of the world economy on Iraq. These historical developments impacted nearly every human society on the planet, but they did not happen evenly or in the same way everywhere. The power of Batatu's analysis lies in his insight into their particular effects on Iraq. In his book he traces how older economic drivers (like handicrafts) and forms of transportation (such as camels and sailing ships) gave way to mass-produced goods and steam ships. Changes in farming methods and new regulations of private property also drove many thousands of people to major cities, where they created a new kind of urban politics.[5]

Exploring the Ideas

Ottoman rule in Iraq was generally believed to be regressive and unchanging, implying that the country's real history only began with the British invasion of 1914.[6] In addition, studies of Iraq tended mainly to highlight the impact of colonialism,* thereby diminishing the impact of Ottoman rule.[7] But Batatu believed Ottoman policies were actually key factors in changing Iraqi society. In Batatu's history, the Ottomans show "repeated attempts … to gather all the means of power into [their] hands, break the cohesion of the tribes, and Ottomanize the town population."[8] Batatu's description of their policies demonstrates the dynamic changes of the Ottoman period that contributed to the country's social structure in the twentieth century. This point of view also emphasizes how the British invasion engaged an already changing society, altering its path—and in many cases not for the better.[9]

While Hourani's studies of "the politics of the notables" focused on the power of an urban elite in the Ottoman era, Batatu shows how Baghdad was, for some time, "despoiled and helpless, [with] river works in ruin … and inanimate and faltering trade."[10] He notes the floods and plagues that Baghdad suffered in the eighteenth and nineteenth centuries, saying, "the city was something like a deathtrap, a 'devourer' of people, and the tribal domain a replenisher."[11] Batatu argues that the real political struggle in Iraq was between "the tribes and the riverine cities, and among the tribes themselves over the food-producing flatlands of the Tigris and Euphrates."[12]

In addition, incorporation into a European empire allowed significant economic and political changes to develop. Batatu shows how this change also redefined the relationship between city and countryside. Over the course of the late nineteenth and early twentieth centuries, Iraq became better connected, both physically and politically, to European empires. First, there were Ottoman attempts to connect Baghdad more effectively to the imperial center at Istanbul. Then after World War I, Iraq was integrated into the British Empire.

The drawing of new political boundaries in the Middle East after World War I ended in 1918 meant not only the drawing of new boundaries, but also the founding of a new state, a new bureaucracy and a new army. The new political boundaries cut age-old ties with regions and cities in what became the modern states of Syria* and Turkey.* At the same time, ideologies of self-determination and resistance to foreign rule, such as nationalism* and socialism,* came to the fore. New ideas combined with significant economic changes. Batatu showed how the exploitation of oil resources encouraged the growth of Iraqi bureaucracy, an expansion of government services, and the creation of a better educated population.

However, economic prosperity did not lead to increased political participation, nor was the wealth spread evenly, a fact that provoked mass political action. Above all, Batatu showed how all of these threads produced what he called "an underlying structural discordance" that brought about "conflicts between the classes … that suffered, and the classes … that benefited from [these] processes."[13] Contemporary commentators might see rising prices or unpopular policies as the immediate causes of uprisings. Batatu suggests, instead, that the real causes lay deeper, in the structure and fabric of society, its classes and institutions.

Overlooked

The Old Social Classes uses a particular methodology, Marxist* class-based analysis, a system regularly used to investigate a range of topics in historical studies.[14] However, he applies this methodology very specifically in terms both of time and place. So while the book remains an indispensable work for readers of Iraqi history, its influence on other studies of other regions is limited. This is because of the unique way Batatu obtained his source material and the nature of Iraq as a newly fabricated state. Nevertheless, it may be argued that the text could be used as a model for social histories of other parts of the Middle East, as Batatu did himself in his examination of Syria.[15]

There are still reasons to examine Batatu's work in the context of larger, global trends, because he depicts an Iraqi society in the grips of major changes—the expansion of capitalism* and European empires. The text is an exhaustive, localized examination of those processes in action. Contemporary readers who are interested in a wide variety of topics will find it valuable to look at Batatu from this perspective.

NOTES

1   Stephen Hemsley Longrigg, *Four Centuries of Modern Iraq* (Oxford: Oxford University Press, 1925), 78.

2   See Peter Sluglett, *Britain in Iraq, 1914–1932* (London: Ithaca Press, 1976).

3   Hourani's conference paper was eventually printed in William R. Polk and Richard L. Chambers, eds., *Beginnings of Modernization in the Middle East: The Nineteenth Century* (Chicago: University of Chicago Press, 1968).

4   Max Weber, *Economy and Society*, ed. Guenther Roth and Claus Wittich (Berkeley, CA: University of California Press, 1978), 1266–7.

5   Hanna Batatu, *The Old Social Classes and the Revolutionary Movements of Iraq: A Study of Iraq's Landed and Commercial Classes and of its Communists, Ba'thists and Free Officers* (Princeton, NJ: Princeton University Press, 1978), 63–152 and 224–318.

6   Longrigg, *Four Centuries of Modern Iraq*.

7   See for instance Majid Khadduri, *Independent Iraq: A Study in Iraqi Politics Since 1932* (London: Oxford University Press, 1951); and Peter Sluglett, *Britain in Iraq, 1914–1932* (London: Ithaca Press, 1976).

8   Batatu, *Old Social Classes*, 22.

9   For instance, Batatu's analysis traces how the British broke with Ottoman imperial practice and facilitated the registration of communal tribal lands in the names of sheikhs and aghas. These tribal leaders, at one time enemies, then became allies in their domination of the masses.

10 Batatu, *Old Social Classes, 78.*

11 Batatu, *Old Social Classes,* 15.

12 Batatu, *Old Social Classes*, 24.

13 Batatu, *Old Social Classes*, 1113–14.

14 The classic volume of Marxist historical analysis is E. P. Thompson's *The Making of the English Working Class* (London: Victor Gollancz, 1963), demonstrating how this mode of inquiry was used to elucidate histories in very different times and places.

15 Hanna Batatu, *Syria's Peasantry, the Descendants of Its Lesser Rural Notables, and Their Politics* (Princeton, NJ: Princeton University Press, 1999).

MODULE 7
ACHIEVEMENT

KEY POINTS

- *The Old Social Classes* offers immense detail on the sweeping historical changes that transformed Iraq* in the twentieth century.

- Batatu's meticulous collection of data, unprecedented access to Iraqi Ministry of Interior files, and use of oral histories and interviews provide the basis for his history of class struggle.

- In the latter part of his book, Batatu investigates contemporary events, which do not benefit from the additional context that only the passage of time can provide.

Assessing the Argument

In *The Old Social Classes and the Revolutionary Movements of Iraq*, Hanna Batatu documents both the long- and short-term factors that resulted in the 1958 revolution in Iraq.* The long-term factors of economic development and the formation of new social classes are particularly well documented. Batatu provides specific detail on the make-up of each social group and how they were affected by capitalism* and economic integration. Some of the short-term factors, such as political protests like 1948's al-Wathbah ("The Leap") and negotiations around the 1955 Baghdad Pact,* are also well documented. Batatu's writing on these topics includes both vigorous descriptions of events and analyses of how the various elements interacted.

In the later chapters on the post-revolution Ba'thist* regimes Batatu relies heavily on interviews for evidence. These sections were

> **❝** [M]y book does not reflect merely my emphasis on structural history which I owe to Marx,* but also some elements of British empiricism,* especially its scrupulous regard for facts and its distrust of large generalizations. There is, I think, a mirroring in my book of the tension between these two intellectual traditions. **❞**
>
> Hanna Batatu, "The Old Social Classes Revisited"

written near the time of publication in 1978 and covered events that happened as late as 1973, just five years previously. Batatu did not have the luxury of the historical perspective that he brought to his discussions of Iraq in the nineteenth century and before World War II.* There, the passing of time reveals what lasted and what did not. However, in the case of Batatu's writing on the Ba'thists, the important events were simply too close to his own time.

Achievement in Context

Opinions differed on how successful Batatu's book was. American and European scholars gave it positive reviews. No work of such scope on twentieth-century Iraq had ever been published in the English language. Reviews of Batatu's text emphasized this time and again. Iraq specialist Abbas Kelidar* commented, "[*The Old Social Classes*] constitutes the most valuable source on the socio-economic politics of the modern state of Iraq ever published."[1] The British Arab historian Peter Sluglett,* meanwhile, noted, "The people of Iraq, to whom the book is dedicated, have a worthy chronicler of their recent past."[2]

The book was received very differently in Iraq itself, however. For many years the Iraqi state stopped the book from being translated into Arabic. For at least five years after publication, the Iraqi government managed to prevent the work from appearing in the country at all. This highlighted the actions of the secretive and authoritarian governments that came to rule the country and their desire to suppress alternative histories of contemporary Iraq.[3]

Limitations

The Old Social Classes focuses almost solely on Iraq and so has not received much attention from scholars working on other parts of the world. Other books on Iraq have concentrated on the history of the British Empire in the Middle East and on the region's international context.[4] In contrast, Batatu only discusses British imperial* policies when they were relevant to events taking place in Iraq. So, while the book has remained a key text in Middle Eastern history, it has not influenced historians and political analysts who focus on regions beyond the Middle East.

Still, Batatu's theories on revolution and the way he handles his evidence mean that Middle East scholars from different academic disciplines have referenced him. His work spans several disciplines and his inspection of social class and use of interviews place him more squarely within social science disciplines such as political science and sociology. However, his archival work and interpretation skills make him more of an historian. This broad disciplinary approach is reflected in the various journals that responded to *The Old Social Classes*. Reviews of the book appeared not only in major Middle East studies journals such as *MERIP Reports*, but also in *American Political Science Review* and *American Journal of Sociology*.[5]

NOTES

1   Abbas Kelidar, review of *The Old Social Classes and the Revolutionary Movements of Iraq: A Study of Iraq's Old Landed and Commercial Classes and of its Communists, Ba'thists and Free Officers,* by Hanna Batatu, *International Affairs* 56 (1980): 741.

2   Peter Sluglett, "Hanna Batatu and Iraqi Politics," *Democratiya* 4 (2006): 18.

3   Joe Stork, review of "Book III: The Communists, Ba'thists and Free
     Officers," in *The Old Social Classes and the Revolutionary Movements
     of Iraq: A Study of Iraq's Old Landed and Commercial Classes and of its
     Communists, Ba'thists and Free Officers*, by Hanna Batatu, *MERIP Reports*
     97 (1981), 32.

4   See, for instance, Reeva Spector Simon, *Iraq Between the Two World Wars:
     The Militarist Origins of Tyranny* (New York: Columbia University Press,
     1986), 7–40; and Charles Tripp, *A History of Iraq* (Cambridge: Cambridge
     University Press, 2000), 30–74.

5   See Stork, "Book III", 22–32; James A. Bill, review of *The Old Social
     Classes and the Revolutionary Movements of Iraq: A Study of Iraq's Old
     Landed and Commercial Classes and of its Communists, Ba'thists and
     Free Officers,* by Hanna Batatu, *The American Political Science Review* 74
     (1980): 529–30; Said Amir Arjomand, review of *The Old Social Classes
     and the Revolutionary Movements of Iraq: A Study of Iraq's Old Landed and
     Commercial Classes and of Its Communists, Ba'thists, and Free Officers*, by
     Hanna Batatu, *American Journal of Sociology* 88 (1982): 469–71.

MODULE 8
PLACE IN THE AUTHOR'S WORK

KEY POINTS

- Hanna Batatu wrote major books examining the political impact of socio-economic transformations in two different Middle Eastern states, Iraq* and Syria.*

- *The Old Social Classes* represents a style of highly detailed and distinctive argument that Batatu then used in his later book on Syria.

- *The Old Social Classes* established Batatu as a leading historian of the twentieth-century Middle East and an important theorist of the effects of socio-economic change on Middle Eastern societies.

Positioning

Hanna Batatu initially intended to write a book examining the working classes in both Syria and Iraq, but soon changed his mind and decided to focus solely on Iraq. His PhD dissertation, "The Shaykh and the Peasant in Iraq, 1917–1958," examined Iraqi social classes in the early twentieth century and Iraq's communist* movement. However, it did not contain any of the material he later published on the period after the 1958 revolution.* Batatu conducted research in Iraq for his dissertation both before and after the 1958 revolution before graduating from Harvard in 1960. During this period, he gained access to previously unseen secret police files and other government documents.[1]

During his time in Beirut after 1962 where he was employed at the American University, Batatu continued to work on *The Old Social Classes and the Revolutionary Movements of Iraq*. He obtained further

> ❝Moreover, what happened in Iraq in 1958 and 1959, and later in 1963—awe-inspiring and terrible events whose course I watched closely and with intense interest—confirmed me in the view that it is in moments of great upheaval that societies are best studied. It seemed, indeed, that at no other moment did Iraqi society bare itself as much or disclose more of its secrets. ❞
>
> Hanna Batatu, "The Old Social Classes Revisited"

access to material on Iraqi leaders after the revolution, such as the Free Officers* and Ba'thists,* and was able to interview communist leaders held in prison at Baqubah to the north of Baghdad.[2] He knew the leader of Iraq, Abd al-Karim Qasim,* who played a leading role in overthrowing the monarchy in 1958 and became the first prime minister of the new Iraqi republic. Batatu added this additional research to his original dissertation and the final product, a work of nearly 1,300 pages divided into three volumes, was published in 1978, more than twenty years after work had begun on it.

Integration

Batatu took up the Shaykh Sabah al-Salem al-Sabah chair in contemporary Arab studies at Georgetown University in Washington, DC in 1982. At his first lecture, he presented his work on Iraq and laid the groundwork for future studies. In this address, which was published in book form in 1984, Batatu noted "there are great gaps in our knowledge of the social origins and social outcomes of Arab revolutions."[3] Work on filling this gap occupied much of Batatu's time at Georgetown.

He completed his only other published book, *Syria's Peasantry, the Descendants of Its Lesser Rural Notables, and Their Politics*, in 1999.[4] Like

The Old Social Classes, it relied heavily on empirical* detail in examining the country's rural population and politics. This work revisited many of the same questions as Batatu's text on Iraq, albeit with a narrower focus on Syria's lower classes. Near the end of his life, Batatu anticipated writing a third text on Palestine,* which would analyze the history of his homeland in the same way. This work was never completed. However, Batatu's two books on Syria and Iraq still provided a social basis for understanding the revolutions that swept the Arab world from the 1950s to the 1970s.

Batatu's work was a major influence on scholars of Iraq and Syria. One of his most important contributions was the vast body of evidence he amassed that would otherwise not exist. By collecting and interpreting such a range of work, Batatu gave scholars of Iraqi and Syrian politics and history invaluable source material.

Significance

Batatu's research and methods did not give rise to a discernable "school," a fact noted by the British historian Roger Owen.* However, his work on Iraq and Syria has provided inspiration and a sizable foundation of detailed research on which historians can build further.[5] Historian Samira Haj,* for example, took up Batatu's Marxist* analytical framework in her text *The Making of Iraq, 1900–1963: Capital, Power, and Ideology*. Haj's work is an investigation into the land tenure system (a set of rules defining how land is to be allocated) and conflicts around land ownership in the creation of the Iraqi state.[6] Similarly, the academic Joseph Sassoon* built on Batatu's early analysis of the Ba'th* Party in his text *Saddam Hussein's Ba'th Party: Inside an Authoritarian Regime*.[7]

Batatu's arguments and analysis have proven to be durable. *The Old Social Classes* still represents the best study on the emergence of a communist party in a Middle Eastern state. Batatu's work also opened up the field of Middle Eastern studies to class-based analysis. Later writers, such as social historians Joel Beinin* and Zachary Lockman,* followed in his footsteps, adopting Batatu's form of analysis in their studies.[8] Overall, Batatu's works illuminate the rural and social history of people living in two states—Iraq and Syria—born from the wreckage of the Ottoman Empire.* These were fabricated states that had for much of the twentieth century been regarded simply as problems of international politics. Batatu's work looked at the problem from a different point of view and addressed the roles played by arbitrary frontiers and the issue of national identity in the turbulent histories of both Iraq and Syria.

NOTES

1   E. Roger Owen, "The Historian as Witness: In Memory of Hanna Batatu (1926–2000)," *Harvard Middle Eastern and Islamic Review* 6 (2000–2001), 95–6.

2   Hanna Batatu, *The Old Social Classes and the Revolutionary Movements of Iraq: A Study of Iraq's Landed and Commercial Classes and of its Communists, Ba'thists and Free Officers* (Princeton, NJ: Princeton University Press, 1978), xxii.

3   Hanna Batatu, *The Egyptian, Syrian, and Iraqi Revolutions: Some Observations on Their Underlying Causes and Social Character* (Washington, DC: Georgetown University Press, 1984), 1.

4   Hanna Batatu, *Syria's Peasantry, the Descendants of Its Lesser Rural Notables, and Their Politics* (Princeton, NJ: Princeton University Press, 1999).

5   Owen, "Historian as Witness," 106.

6   Samira Haj, *The Making of Iraq, 1900–1963: Capital, Power, and Ideology* (Albany, NY: SUNY Press, 1997).

7   Joseph Sassoon, *Saddam Hussein's Ba'th Party: Inside an Authoritarian Regime* (Cambridge: Cambridge University Press, 2012).

8   Joel Beinin and Zachary Lockman, *Workers on the Nile: Nationalism, Communism, Islam and the Egyptian Working Class, 1882–1954* (Princeton, NJ: Princeton University Press, 1987).

SECTION 3
IMPACT

THE FIRST RESPONSES

KEY POINTS

- Early assessments of Hanna Batatu's book focused on its readability and its theoretical contributions.

- While *The Old Social Classes* overturned the notion that socio-economic classes* were not a valuable frame of analysis, critics suggested he may have exaggerated the role of class-based politics in the Middle East.

- *The Old Social Classes* presented the history of Iraq,* a previously little-known country, with groundbreaking detail. The book was a revelation for Western scholars and this shaped their reaction to it.

Criticism

Early reactions to *The Old Social Classes and the Revolutionary Movements of Iraq* focused on the novelty of Hanna Batatu's historical sources and the detail of his text. Nearly all of the reviews included comments regarding the "sheer scale of [Batatu's] enterprise" and "incredible wealth of detail."[1] One reviewer noted, "Iraqi political patterns have long been a mystery to outsiders who have been forced to interpret events in that country largely through uninformed and distorted reports sporadically presented by the mass media."[2] Batatu's major contribution was to bring to light the politics and history of a country that were unknown in the English language. Indeed, this was a politics and history that had barely been chronicled within Iraq itself.[3]

The critics did find fault, though, with Batatu's writing style and theoretical structure. International Studies professor James A. Bill*

> **❝** Hanna Batatu has constructed a masterpiece of historical literature that singlehandedly catapults Iraq from the least known of the major Arab countries to the Arab society of which we now have the most thorough political portrait. **❞**
>
> Joe Stork,* review of *The Old Social Classes*

found that at times the text was "extremely repetitious" and "the conceptual and theoretical underpinnings … somewhat shaky and at times inconsistently applied."[4] However, Bill also noted that Batatu's "shaky" application meant he could avoid "straight description and enumeration" in favor of analyses "at the medium level" that would not have fit within a more rigid theoretical framework. Marion Farouk-Sluglett* and Peter Sluglett,* who both wrote books and articles on Iraq, took Batatu to task on a different theoretical point. The Slugletts felt that Batatu relied too heavily on "social condition" in looking at the appeal of communism.* They write that Batatu "seems to overestimate the direct relationship between poverty and hardship and revolutionary consciousness." In their opinion, the formulation is too simplistic and "deprivation and hardship *alone*, without political education and organization, do not create movements of revolutionary change."[5]

Responses

Batatu appears to have anticipated at least some of the criticisms of his work and he addressed them directly. He was aware both of his particular writing style and the extraordinary amount of detail he included in the book. As he said in the preface, "Perhaps the exposition lapses here and there into minutiae or verges on scholarly overkill."[6] Batatu defends this style, though, noting that "the patient reader" will realize how much depended "on personal and accidental factors" that only a detailed approach could explain. In fact, Batatu's insistence on including as much detail as possible resulted in a long struggle with his publisher, Princeton University Press, who had wanted a shorter text.[7]

In other cases, Batatu made no direct response. He often brushed aside criticisms of his theoretical argument or distanced himself from a strict interpretation of theory. In an interview shortly after the publication of *The Old Social Classes*, he made it clear that he had not intended to slavishly imitate either Karl Marx* or Max Weber.* He said the ideas laid out by these theorists were "helpful in the reading of historical situations"—implying that a strict theoretical model had never been his intention.[8]

Conflict and Consensus

Critiques of Batatu's emphasis on the effects of socio-economic class* on Iraq's history continued to hound the author. Marion Farouk-Sluglett and Peter Sluglett, for instance, suggested there were other loyalties and ties beyond social class that affected social behavior in Iraqi society.[9] Additionally, events in Iraq later in the twentieth century challenged some of Batatu's analysis. The rise of Saddam Hussein* to become President of Iraq in 1979 and the viciousness of some of his Ba'thist* policies called into question the way Batatu presented the Ba'th in his book. Batatu accounted for Ba'thist repression in the early 1970s as an initial "insecurity" in the regime, not as an ongoing feature of Ba'thist rule.[10]

Batatu continued to insist that material factors—the ownership of land or money income—played a pivotal role in the outcome of Iraqi history.[11] When it came to the Ba'th, he made some criticism of Saddam Hussein's regime, but never fully discredited the Ba'th Party.* At a conference in Britain about Baghdad's repression of the Shi'i* population in Iraq, Batatu described an important Shi'i cleric and resistance leader as a "martyr." This provoked an angry response from the Iraqis in the audience, who were sympathetic to the regime.

Batatu's decision to avoid outright condemnation of the Ba'th may have been tactical. He wanted to continue his research in Iraq while the Ba'thists were in power and even conducted fieldwork in Saddam Hussein's hometown of Tikrit in 1982.[12]

NOTES

1   These quotes are taken from Marion Farouk-Sluglett and Peter Sluglett, review of "Book II: The Communists and Their Movement," and Joe Stork, review of "Book III: The Communists, Ba'thists and Free Officers," in *The Old Social Classes and the Revolutionary Movements of Iraq: A Study of Iraq's Old Landed and Commercial Classes and of its Communists, Ba'thists and Free Officers*, by Hanna Batatu, *MERIP Reports* 97 (1981): 27 and 31, respectively.

2   James A. Bill, review of *The Old Social Classes and the Revolutionary Movements of Iraq: A Study of Iraq's Old Landed and Commercial Classes and of its Communists, Ba'thists and Free Officers,* by Hanna Batatu, *The American Political Science Review* 74 (1980): 529.

3   Farouk-Sluglett and Sluglett, "Book II," 27.

4   Bill, "Review," 530.

5   Farouk-Sluglett and Sluglett, "Book II," 27.

6   Hanna Batatu, *The Old Social Classes and the Revolutionary Movements of Iraq: A Study of Iraq's Landed and Commercial Classes and of its Communists, Ba'thists and Free Officers* (Princeton, NJ: Princeton University Press, 1978), xxi.

7   E. Roger Owen, "The Historian as Witness: In Memory of Hanna Batatu (1926–2000)," *Harvard Middle Eastern and Islamic Review* 6 (2000–2001): 98.

8   Hanna Batatu, Philip Khoury, and Joe Stork, "Hanna Batatu's Achievement: A Faithful History of the Class Struggle in Iraq," *MERIP Reports* 97 (1981): 22.

9   Marion Farouk-Sluglett and Peter Sluglett, "The Social Classes and the Origins of the Revolution," in *The Iraqi Revolution of 1958: The Old Social Classes Revisited*, ed. Robert A. Fernea and Wm. Roger Louis (London: I.B. Tauris, 1991), 133. Roger A. Owen also brings up similar issues in his chapter in the same volume, "Class and Class Politics in Iraq before 1958: The 'Colonial and Post-Colonial State,'" 154–5.

10 Peter Sluglett, "Hanna Batatu and Iraqi Politics," *Democratiya* 4 (2006): 9; Batatu, *The Old Social Classes*, 1093.

11 Hanna Batatu, "The Old Social Classes Revisited," in *The Iraqi Revolution of 1958: The Old Social Classes Revisited*, ed. Robert A. Fernea and W. Roger Louis (London: I.B. Tauris, 1991), 217–18.

12 Owen, "Historian as Witness," 102.

MODULE 10
THE EVOLVING DEBATE

KEY POINTS

- Hanna Batatu continued to be criticized on three major fronts: his lack of attention to the structure of the colonial state, an exaggeration of the social effects of economic change, and an inexplicable approval of the Ba'th Party.*

- *The Old Social Classes* fostered new scholarly works and debates on the historical role and significance of the Iraqi Communist Party* and the Ba'th Party.

- Despite its limitations *The Old Socials Classes* remains a hugely important work because of its scope, its attention to detail, and its sources.

Uses and Problems

In March 1989, a group of Middle East scholars including Rashid Khalidi,* Peter Sluglett,* William Roger Louis,* and Roger Owen* met at the University of Texas at Austin to discuss the Iraqi revolution of 1958.* The group paid particular attention to Hanna Batatu's *The Old Social Classes and the Revolutionary Movements of Iraq*. Their discussions showed how Batatu's work continued to be useful ten years after its publication.[1]

Overall, Batatu's contemporaries focused on problems of context rather than content, for instance the limitations of structuralism.* This is the school of thought that believes there is an underlying architecture to human activities and a system of interrelations that can be both understood and described. Louis and Khalidi emphasized the importance of the international arena to the revolution. Louis suggested that particular political problems immediately preceding the

> **❝** I do not see him [Batatu] as a political scientist in the contemporary sense of the term, but more as someone who began his research by writing in the tradition of those intellectually self-confident, late eighteenth- and early nineteenth-century thinkers who imagined the possibility of a science of society based on the tools provided by political economy. **❞**
>
> E. Roger Owen, "Historian as Witness"

revolution were important, too, such as the contested 1955 negotiations with Britain over the Baghdad Pact,* a mutual defense treaty that also included Iraq,* Iran, Turkey, and Pakistan.[2] Khalidi argued that major events in the Arab world were also vital in understanding the Iraqi experience, particularly those in Egypt, such as the 1952 revolution* and the subsequent Suez Crisis* of 1956.[3] The Suez Canal ran through Egyptian territory connecting the Red Sea to the Mediterranean. Egyptian President Gamal Abdel Nasser* wanted to assert Egyptian sovereignty over the canal and obtain additional revenue, so he nationalized the canal company in 1956. Arguing that nationalization threatened a vital trade route, Israel,* France, and Britain invaded Egypt. They were later forced to withdraw from under intense pressure from both the Soviet Union* and the United States.

Owen, on the other hand, argued that Batatu's focus on socio-economic classes* had left the colonial state out of the analysis and suggested ways to "bring the state back in."[4] For Owen, struggle between social groups was important, but equally important were the deficiencies in the state created by the British. According to Owen, the Iraqi government under the influence of the British "deliberately brought about the entry of a number of social groups into the political arena without providing a set of satisfactory mechanisms by which their various interests and demands could be reconciled … or contained."[5]

Peter Sluglett and his wife, Marion Farouk-Sluglett,* delivered the sharpest criticism of Batatu's work, attacking his central assertion that Iraq's incorporation into the global capitalist* system had entirely altered Iraqi society. They believed too little was known about "the degree to which [pre-capitalist] relations were transformed or replaced, or to what extent they [the Iraqi peasantry] merely adapted themselves to the new socio-economic conditions while retaining many of their original features."[6] In other words, they questioned Batatu's conclusions about the extent of the changes that economic integration had brought. They also argued that the staunch identification of Iraqis with Islam* meant the major secular political movements at the center of the 1958 revolution did not represent the country as a whole. Later developments in Iraqi politics suggest the Slugletts were largely correct. Political movements driven by religion became much more important in the decades following the 1958 revolution. For instance, Shi'i* political organizations, such as the Islamic Dawa Party* and the Supreme Council for the Islamic Revolution in Iraq,* played significant roles in providing later opposition to the Ba'thist regime of Saddam Hussein.*

Schools of Thought

Batatu's text has had limited influence outside the field of Iraqi history. Owen noted that Batatu's "style of collecting evidence … is so particular to him that it seems unlikely that it will ever be imitated … Batatu … ranged far beyond the usual libraries and interviews … to include the fields, the factories, and the prisons where history was also being made."[7] While primarily a historian, in a sense Batatu also functioned very well as an ethnologist* and sociologist.* His unique qualities, and even the way in which he presents his work, make it difficult to place him within a specific discipline.

It is, in fact, unclear what influence he may have had on those Middle East historians who were part of the social history movement of the 1960s and 1970s—scholars such as Joel Beinin* and Zachary Lockman.* *The Old Social Classes* has clearly generated further Marxist* analysis of Iraq, including books such as Samira Haj's* *The Making of Iraq, 1900–1963,* which relies heavily on Batatu's collection of data.[8] *The Old Social Classes* has also paved the way for narrower studies, such as Tareq Ismael's* *The Rise and Fall of the Communist Party of Iraq*[9] and Johan Franzén's* *Red Star Over Iraq.*[10] Both expand on Batatu's analysis of the Iraqi Communist Party. While a revered scholar and influential in the field of Iraqi history, Batatu's wider application and impact remains relatively limited.

In Current Scholarship

The Old Social Classes remains the definitive social history of Iraq in the twentieth century because of its scope, attention to detail, and unique set of sources. Batatu had access to secret police files, political prisoners, and many prominent leaders. Batatu's archival work is particularly important as several important Iraqi libraries were looted and burned during the American invasion and occupation of Baghdad in 2003. As a result carrying forward Batatu's legacy is difficult, if not impossible. Still, historians have taken up his research subjects, even if they have not carried forward his method of analysis. Recent books on the Iraqi Communist Party and the Ba'th Party have built on Batatu's research.[11] Nevertheless, *The Old Social Classes* remains a unique testament to the political and social struggles of Iraq.

Writers of Iraqi history need to approach Batatu almost as if he were a primary, rather than a secondary source. His contribution is extremely important, as the most widely used primary sources on this period in Iraqi history are British and American archives.[12] Batatu did use British sources, but his text also includes a great deal of evidence from Iraq itself. Batatu's recording of these voices makes the book an important source in its own right.

For a book like Batatu's, the important measure is not whether he brought about a school of thought—which he did not—or whether his book has been superseded—which it has not. What is important is whether it remains a vital touchstone for the writing of Iraqi history. In that sense, it has succeeded beyond measure. Even as scholars criticize Batatu's characterizations or interpretations, they still use his evidence. The book is a treasure trove for scholars of Iraq because Batatu reveals details on an immense number of topics. His book still stimulates more questions than he himself could possibly have answered and represents a rite of passage for anyone thinking about writing on Iraq.

NOTES

1 The essays are collected in a volume, Robert A. Fernea and Wm. Roger Louis, eds., *The Iraqi Revolution of 1958: The Old Social Classes Revisited* (London: I. B. Tauris, 1991).

2 Wm. Roger Louis, "The British and the Origins of the Iraqi Revolution," in *The Iraqi Revolution of 1958*, ed. Fernea and Louis, 39–41.

3 Rashid Khalidi, "The Impact of the Iraqi Revolution," in *The Iraqi Revolution of 1958*, ed. Fernea and Louis, 116–17.

4 Roger Owen, "Class and Class Politics in Iraq before 1958: The 'Colonial and Post-Colonial State'," in *The Iraqi Revolution of 1958*, ed. Fernea and Louis, 155. See also Roger Owen, *State, Power and Politics in the Making of the Modern Middle East* (London: Routledge, 1992).

5 Owen, "Class and Class Politics," 157.

6 Marion Farouk-Sluglett and Peter Sluglett, "The Social Classes and the Origins of the Revolution," in *The Iraqi Revolution of 1958*, ed. Fernea and Louis, 136.

7 E. Roger Owen, "The Historian as Witness: In Memory of Hanna Batatu (1926–2000)," *Harvard Middle Eastern and Islamic Review* 6 (2000–2001): 106.

8 Samira Haj, *The Making of Iraq, 1900–1963: Capital, Power, and Ideology* (Albany, NY: SUNY Press, 1997).

9 Tareq Y. Ismael, *The Rise and Fall of the Communist Party of Iraq* (New York: Cambridge University Press, 2008).

10 Johan Franzén, *Red Star Over Iraq: The Iraqi Communist Party and the Evolution of Ideological Politics in Pre-Saddam Iraq* (New York: Columbia University Press, 2011).

11 These works include Ismael, *The Rise and Fall of the Communist Party of Iraq*; Franzén, *Red Star Over Iraq*; and Joseph Sassoon, *Saddam Hussein's Ba'th Party: Inside an Authoritarian Regime* (Cambridge: Cambridge University Press, 2012).

12 Marion Farouk-Sluglett and Peter Sluglett, "The Historiography of Modern Iraq," *American Historical Review* 96 (1991): 1408.

IMPACT AND INFLUENCE TODAY

KEY POINTS

- *The Old Social Classes* remains the definitive social history of Iraq* in the twentieth century. It was republished in 2004 and is regularly cited by scholars of modern Iraq.

- Batatu's emphasis on the economic and material basis of social and political change contrasts with those who prefer to stress cultural or political factors.

- Some scholars have criticized Batatu's interpretation of events as too rigid and too influenced by Marxist* models.

Position

As "the most detailed modern history available on any Arab country," Hanna Batatu's *The Old Social Classes and the Revolutionary Movements of Iraq* is still extremely relevant for scholars of Iraq and the Middle East generally.[1] Batatu's new social history,* though, did give way to other forms of historical inquiry. Following the end of the Cold War* in 1991, Marxist analyses of social structure became less relevant. From the 1980s and 1990s there was increased interest in the development of modern political Islam,* a term used to describe a range of religious and political ideologies, all based on the idea that the religion of Islam should guide the political life of a community. As a result, new histories have been written exploring the social, political, and economic impact of religious leaders and communities in Iraq. These include works by historians Pierre-Jean Luizard* and Yitzhak Nakash* on the Shi'i* communities.[2] Other works by scholars such as Orit Bashkin* have focused on Iraq's intellectual

> 66 *The Old Social Classes* is an inspired and inspiring book, a work of passionate commitment and profound scholarship. It provokes many questions on the writing of contemporary history, and the relation of the historian to his human and documentary material. 99
>
> Peter Sluglett, "Hanna Batatu and Iraqi Politics"

history.[3] But even as scholars have moved away from Batatu's style of class-based analysis, they continue to draw from his work.

Batatu's efforts are also still relevant because Iraq has been at the forefront of world affairs so much in the last 25 years. The American-led incursion in the Gulf War* of 1991 and the invasion during the Iraq War* of 2003 generated an enormous amount of journalism and military histories with varying levels of awareness of Iraq's history and social structure.[4] Saqi Books republished *The Old Social Classes* in 2004 as a result of renewed interest in Iraq. Batatu's text still stands as an important source for anyone seeking to understand Iraqi history and the initial rise of the Ba'th Party.*[5]

Interaction

The Old Social Classes is still relevant today because it challenges the works of contemporary thinkers who use Iraqi history as a testing ground for ideas about empire. Batatu sees economic conditions as the driving force of history and he investigates how these conditions change across a broad spectrum of Iraqi social groups. At the root of his arguments about the long-term causes of revolution is the idea that Iraqis made their own history and it was economic conditions that determined social and political groupings.

This view of Iraqi history challenges those who make empire and the colonial state the determining factors. Historian Priya

Satia's* *Spies in Arabia: The Great War and the Cultural Foundations of Britain's Covert Empire in the Middle East* paints a picture of an Iraq dominated by a "covert empire" where the British created "a parallel state, entirely informal and in the hands of intelligence officers who held real executive power."[6] According to Satia, "particular intelligence and military practices and, ultimately, a particular kind of imperial state emerged from a particular cultural construction of the Middle East."[7]

While it is worth noting that Satia's main focus is British imperial* practice and not Iraqi social history, it is difficult to believe the two books are discussing the same location and time. Satia's work implies that Batatu's story of the economic impact of empire and policies designed to make Iraq into a governable space by real means was not actually happening at all. Instead, she believes British intelligence officers, with a peculiarly British understanding of the Middle East, created an entirely separate mechanism to control the country. Meanwhile, scholars such as Rashid Khalidi* and Roger Owen* have criticized Batatu's work for not dealing with the international arena and the colonial state. His research, though, provides an alternative to histories that in effect diminish the role Iraqis themselves played in shaping the destiny of their own country.[8]

The Continuing Debate

Recent books, such as political scientist Charles Tripp's* *A History of Iraq*, have taken advantage of Batatu's rich detail to provide a more accessible work for general readers.[9] However, some scholars have taken Batatu to task in recent years over the rigid approach of his analysis. They suggest the author tried to shape Iraqi history according to the Marxist* model. Orit Bashkin's *The Other Iraq: Pluralism and Culture in Hashemite Iraq* uses *The Old Social Classes* for its rich store of information but questions Batatu's interpretation.

Bashkin criticizes Batatu's method of communicating "his notions about the 'correct' ways in which Iraqi intellectuals ought to have interpreted Marxism and socialism."* Bashkin suggests "he missed an opportunity to explore how the translations and adaptations of such theories in the Iraqi context produced new and interesting cultural models."[10] The implication is not that Batatu's content was *wrong*, but that his attachment to Marxist models blinded him to certain other factors.

Peter Sluglett,* meanwhile, criticizes Batatu for his characterization of the Ba'thist movement, saying "I find it hard to understand … what positive elements he could ever have found in Ba'thism, or perhaps more accurately why he was not more clearly aware of the farrago of nonsense, mostly poisonous nonsense, that it now seems (and to me at least, has always seemed) to be."[11] Sluglett argues that much of Batatu's discussion of Ba'thism is "something of a disappointment" because the author's "rather ambivalent attitude towards Ba'thism" undermines his "profound sympathy with the 'real left'."[12] As an example, Sluglett points to Saddam Hussein's* invasion of Iran in 1980. The Islamic Revolution* a year earlier had overthrown the American-backed Shah of Iran, Mohammad Reza Pahlavi.* Saddam Hussein made himself an agent of the United States in trying to contain Iran and this act, Sluglett says, "put paid once and for all to the image he [Hussein] had tried to create for himself as a crusader for Arabism against imperialism." Yet even then Batatu did not condemn the Iraqi Ba'th for their hypocrisy.[13] Sluglett puts this response down to some kind of commitment on Batatu's part to Arab solidarity. Perhaps Batatu held out hope that the socialist* ideology of Ba'thist thinkers would eventually triumph in the halls of Arab governments. However, as subsequent events in the country confirmed, Sluglett had good reason to point out the problems in Batatu's portrayal of the Ba'th.

NOTES

1 Tom Nieuwenhuis, review of "Book 1: The Old Social Classes," in *The Old Social Classes and the Revolutionary Movements of Iraq: A Study of Iraq's Old Landed and Commercial Classes and of its Communists, Ba'thists and Free Officers*, by Hanna Batatu, *MERIP Reports* 97 (1981): 22, 24, 25.

2 Pierre-Jean Luizard, *La Formation de l'Irak Contemporain: le Rôle Politique des Ulémas Chiites à la Fin de la Domination Ottomane et au Moment de la Construction de l'Etat Irakien* (Paris: Editions du Centre National de la Recherche Scientifique, 1991); and Yitzhak Nakash, *The Shi'is of Iraq* (Princeton, NJ: Princeton University Press, 1994).

3 Orit Bashkin, *The Other Iraq: Pluralism and Culture in Hashemite Iraq* (Stanford, CA: Stanford University Press, 2009).

4 Some examples include Nir Rosen, *Aftermath: Following the Bloodshed of America's Wars in the Muslim World* (New York: Nation Books, 2010) and Tony Horowitz, *Baghdad Without a Map and Other Misadventures in Arabia* (New York: Plume, 1991).

5 Peter Sluglett, "Hanna Batatu and Iraqi Politics," *Democratiya* 4 (2006): 7, 17–18.

6 Priya Satia, *Spies in Arabia: The Great War and the Cultural Foundations of Britain's Covert Empire in the Middle East* (New York: Oxford University Press, 2008), 7.

7 Satia, *Spies in Arabia*, 10.

8 For critiques of Batatu's text, see Rashid Khalidi, "The Impact of the Iraqi Revolution on the Arab World," and Roger Owen, "Class and Class Politics in Iraq before 1958: the 'Colonial and Post-Colonial State,'" in *The Iraqi Revolution of 1958: The Old Social Classes Revisited*, ed. Robert A. Fernea and Wm. Roger Louis (London: I. B. Tauris, 1991), 106–17 and 154–71, respectively.

9 Charles Tripp, *A History of Iraq* (Cambridge: Cambridge University Press, 2000), 112–13 and 118–19.

10 Bashkin, *The Other Iraq*, 13.

11 Sluglett, "Hanna Batatu and Iraqi Politics," 9.

12 Sluglett, "Hanna Batatu and Iraqi Politics," 9.

13 Sluglett, "Hanna Batatu and Iraqi Politics," 9.

WHERE NEXT?

KEY POINTS

- *The Old Social Classes* continues to be used by scholars of modern Iraq* as both a reference and intellectual benchmark.

- No other history of Iraq provides a similar level of detail as Batatu's. This has created the potential for any number of future research projects.

- The text is a seminal piece of history on the Middle East and adds greatly to a general understanding of how global economic integration affected social and political life in a major Middle Eastern state.

Potential

Hanna Batatu's *The Old Social Classes and the Revolutionary Movements of Iraq* is still a key text for future historians of Iraq because of its wide variety of archival and oral history—both British and Iraqi—and its descriptive detail. Moreover, Batatu puts Iraqi actors and their motivations in the foreground of Iraqi history. This is one way in which his writing of Iraqi history differs from the work of other scholars on Iraq.[1] Because they were not able to travel to Iraq or access the type of archival materials Batatu did, other historians have often written their accounts of the country based on American or British perspectives. These countries' archives are still open, unlike Iraq's.[2]

While some of the concerns of new social history* are still being pursued—as in the work of gender historian Sara Pursley*—it is unclear whether there will be a revival of Batatu's version of class-based analysis.[3] *The Old Social Classes'* potential, therefore, lies more in its use as a point of reference and for context. It offers a rich

> **"** *The Old Social Classes* immediately became something
> of a 'Bible' for everyone working in modern Iraqi history,
> as well as constituting a significant political intervention
> in its own right. It also contains enough information
> to write countless other versions of the same history
> focusing on areas which Batatu himself only touched on
> or, in some cases, left out almost entirely. **"**
>
> E. Roger Owen, "Historian as Witness"

background of information with which to look at new questions
about Iraq, such as the effects of recent wars. New scholarship is
unlikely to sideline Batatu's work entirely, though it may raise further
points of contention with his characterization of events and their
causes. The scope and detail of Batatu's work will make sure it
remains useful in developing any future histories of Iraq.

Future Directions

Batatu's work still leaves many potentially fruitful avenues open and
The Old Social Classes is particularly useful in providing context for
new historical investigations. For example, scholars such as Charles
Townshend* and Arbella Bet-Shlimon* are delving deeper into Iraq's
World War I* history and the history of its petroleum industry,
respectively.[4]

The Old Social Classes should also benefit those who are beginning
to explore new angles in Iraqi and Middle Eastern history. This is
particularly evident in science and technology studies and environmental
history. These two fields both focus on material conditions, an
important part of Batatu's argument. Science and technology studies
detail the social, political, and cultural context of scientific research and
technology, while environmental history focuses on human engagement
with the natural world. Given Batatu's focus on the material aspect of

social history, new works in these fields can build on the quantity and quality of detail in his text, while using their own frameworks of analysis to ask new questions. Both of these disciplines have received greater attention from those involved in Middle Eastern studies in recent years and it is only a matter of time before they include Iraq more specifically.[5]

Summary

The Old Social Classes represents an unparalleled achievement in Iraqi history and has added greatly to our understanding of the modern Middle East. By obtaining access to secret police files and interviewing major political figures and party leaders, Batatu collected and analyzed an unsurpassed range of documentary and verbal material on Iraqi history and politics.

Within academic circles, the book represents an unrivalled source for further research, as well as a challenge to take Iraqi voices and points of view seriously. Batatu was himself a successful teacher and transmitted his ideas about Middle Eastern history to student activists and leaders.[6] While his scholarship may not have produced a particularly "Batatu" method of social analysis, it was nonetheless embodied in those he educated in Beirut.

Batatu's text is little known outside the relatively limited group of scholars who are concerned with Iraqi history. This is unfortunate, though understandable. The text is quirky in a number of ways. Its long title, which may "seem rather quaint," is aimed at precision. Its level of description, including its 175 tables, often pages long, had a "paralyzing" effect on the author and sometimes leaves the text without a focused argument.[7] Yet it remains extremely important, due in large part to the way that the Iraqi nation became caught up in superpower struggles and is still closely tied to American power after the invasion of 2003. As Batatu makes very clear, Iraq was not created out of nothing. The country's history prior to the British occupation and Mandate of the 1920s had a significant effect on how it developed in the later twentieth century. In the twenty-first century, Iraq's government was obliterated by military conquest, occupied by a coalition of nations led by America, and was then recreated again through American nation-building efforts. These facts re-engage Batatu's history and give it not only continued, but also new, meaning.

NOTES

1   Scholars such as Peter Sluglett, Toby Dodge, and Reeva Spector Simon have written books on Iraq, but their archival resources are primarily American or British. See Peter Sluglett, *Britain in Iraq, 1914–1932* (London: Ithaca Press, 1976); Toby Dodge, *Inventing Iraq: The Failure of Nation Building and a History Denied* (New York: Columbia University Press, 2003); Reeva Spector Simon, *Iraq Between the Two World Wars: The Militarist Origins of Tyranny* (New York: Columbia University Press, 1986).

2   See, for example, political histories that seek to explain British rule in Iraq, such as Priya Satia, *Spies in Arabia: The Great War and the Cultural Foundations of Britain's Covert Empire in the Middle East* (New York: Oxford University Press, 2008); and Matthew Elliot, *'Independent Iraq': The Monarchy and British Influence, 1941–1958* (London: Tauris Academic Studies, 1996). Eliot includes several published sources in Arabic.

3   Sara Pursley, "Daughters of the Right Path: Family Law, Homosocial Publics, and the Ethics of Intimacy in the Works of Shi'i Revivalist Bint al-Huda," *Journal of Middle East Women's Studies* 8 (2012): 51–77.

4   Charles Townshend, *Desert Hell: The British Invasion of Mesopotamia* (Cambridge: Belknap Press, 2010); Arbella Bet-Shlimon, "Group Identities, Oil, and the Local Political Domain in Kirkuk: A Historical Perspective," *Journal of Urban History* 38 (2012): 914–31.

5   See, for example, Timothy Mitchell, *Carbon Democracy: Political Power in the Age of Oil* (New York: Verso, 2011); and Diana K. Davis, *Resurrecting the Granary of Rome: Environmental History and French Colonial Expansion in North Africa* (Athens, OH: Ohio University Press, 2007).

6   E. Roger Owen, "The Historian as Witness: In Memory of Hanna Batatu (1926–2000)," *Harvard Middle Eastern and Islamic Review* 6 (2000–2001): 97.

7   Hanna Batatu, *The Old Social Classes and the Revolutionary Movements of Iraq: A Study of Iraq's Landed and Commercial Classes and of its Communists, Ba'thists and Free Officers* (Princeton, NJ: Princeton University Press, 1978), IX–XVI.

GLOSSARY

GLOSSARY OF TERMS

Arab exceptionalism: a set of theories that sought to differentiate the Arab Middle East from other global trends, including both the rise of communist states and later waves of democratization after the collapse of the communist bloc.

Arab–Israeli War (1948): a war that began on 15 May 1948 as a result of Israel's declaration of independence. The war was a conflict between the Arab nations of Egypt, Jordan, Syria, and Iraq—joined by local Palestinian Arab forces—against the forces of the newly declared State of Israel.

Arab nationalism: refers to the belief that Arabic-speaking peoples share a common heritage and should be part of a single nation-state.

Arab socialism: a combination of ideas bringing together Arab nationalism and socialism. Coined by Syrian thinker Michel Aflaq, the concept of Arab socialism put forward an Arab nationalist idea that all Arabic-speaking peoples belonged to the same nation, together with a moderate socialist idea of social justice and a struggle against the ruling classes.

Atheist: a person who does not believe in the existence of a "supreme being" or god.

Baghdad Pact: later known as the Central Treaty Organization (CENTO). Like the North Atlantic Treaty Organization (NATO), the Pact was an anti-Soviet security agreement and military alliance. Sponsored by the United Kingdom and the United States, it initially included Iran, Iraq, Turkey, Pakistan, and the United Kingdom as members.

Ba'thism: comes from the word *ba'th* in Arabic, meaning "renaissance." An ideology based on the writings of Syrian thinkers Michel Aflaq and Salah ad-Din al-Bitar, Ba'thism espouses the concept of the rebirth of the Arab nation through economic, social, and political progress.

British Mandate of Iraq: Great Britain occupied Iraq during World War I and subsequently obtained a "mandate" from the League of Nations to rule Iraq. This "mandate" was dissolved in 1932 when Iraq was admitted to the League of Nations.

Capitalism: an economic mode in which property and capital goods are privately owned and economic production is aimed at profit.

Cold War (1947–91): a period of high political tension from roughly 1947 to 1991, between a group of countries known as the Western bloc, which included the United States and its European allies, and the Eastern bloc, a group of nations including the Soviet Union and its European allies.

Communism: a political theory and economic ideology derived from the writings of Karl Marx that advocates the collective ownership of property and social revolution ending in a classless society.

Congress: the national legislative body of the United States, comprising the Senate and the House of Representatives.

Decolonization: refers to the overturning of colonial control in a state dependent on an outside power. Decolonization may be understood in a political sense, as attaining independence, and in a cultural sense, as the removal of colonial social and cultural effects.

Democracy: a system of government where all eligible members of the population participate in government, usually through elected representatives.

Egyptian revolution (1952): led by a group of army officers, including Muhammad Naguib and Gamal Abdel Nasser, the revolution abolished the monarchy, established a republic, and ended British influence in Egypt.

Eisenhower Doctrine (1957): American President Dwight D. Eisenhower in an address to the American Congress promulgated the Eisenhower Doctrine on January 5, 1957. In this address, Eisenhower stated that any country threatened by armed aggression could call upon American assistance and military aid.

Empiricism: the idea that all knowledge should be gained by experience, by using experiments and observation to gather facts.

English Civil War (1642–51): involved several conflicts between supporters of the English monarch and those supporting Parliament. The conflict established parliamentary consent over the monarchy and ended the monopoly of the Church of England over religious affairs.

Ethnologist: a person who studies ethnology, the investigation of different peoples and the differences between peoples.

Free Officers Movement: a clandestine group of Iraqi military officers of various political affiliations who were inspired by the Free Officers Movement in Egypt that eventually brought Gamal Abdel Nasser to power in that country. The Iraqi Free Officers were inspired by ideas of pan-Arabism, the concept that all Arabs should be part of one state. They sought to depose what they viewed as a corrupt regime imposed by imperialists.

French Revolution (1789–99): a decade of significant social and political change in France. The revolution was driven by Enlightenment ideals of freedom and equality as well as liberal and radical ideologies and had a profound impact on governance in Europe.

Gulf War (1990–1): The American invasion of Iraq in 1991, also known as the Gulf War, was a conflict between a United Nations-authorized coalition led by the United States against Iraq in response to Iraq's invasion of Kuwait.

Imperialism: a system of rule based on concepts of dominion and superiority whereby one society dominates the territory, as well as the political, social, and economic life, of another society.

Industrial Revolution: a series of economic and social changes brought about by a shift in energy use by human populations, whereby new energy sources such as water and steam power made it possible to develop new machines and manufacturing processes. It began in England in the eighteenth century and later spread to Western Europe and the United States.

Interventionism: a term used to describe the interference of a country or other political entity in another country's affairs, with the implication of achieving a particular outcome.

Iran–Iraq War (1980–8): the longest conventional conflict of the twentieth century began when Iraq invaded Iran on 22 September. The war was a result of ongoing disputes over borders and Iraq's concern for the effect of the Islamic Revolution in Iran (1979) on its majority Shi'i population.

Iraq: a modern state roughly corresponding to three former provinces of the Ottoman Empire, which was defeated at the end of World War I. After the war, the territory was awarded to Britain as a League of Nations Mandate. The country occupies a position at the western end of the Persian Gulf, with its capital Baghdad.

Iraq revolt (1920): uprising that aimed to dislodge the British occupation and establish an independent Arab state and government. While both Shi'i and Sunni groups in Iraq co-operated in the revolt, the British use of air power proved decisive in putting an end to the insurrection, which claimed thousands of lives.

Iraq revolution (1958): a military coup d'état against the British-imposed Hashemite monarchy on 14 July. The revolution overthrew the monarchy and ended British power in the country.

Iraq War (2003–11): invasion of Iraq in 2003 conducted by a coalition of 21 nations led by the United States. The invasion was justified as a response to non-compliance by the Iraqi leader, Saddam Hussein, with respect to his weapons programs. However, no significant evidence of ongoing production of weapons of mass destruction was found in Iraq after the invasion.

Iraqi Ba'th Party: founded by Fuad al-Rikabi in the early 1950s and came to power in Iraq in 1963 through a military coup d'état. The party adhered to the concept of the rebirth of the Arab nation through economic, social, and political progress, an ideology based on the writings of Syrian thinkers Michel Aflaq and Salah ad-Din al-Bitar.

Iraqi Communist Party: founded by Hussein ar-Rahhal, a student of law in Baghdad, who began a study group in 1924 devoted to the writings of Karl Marx. With the global economic downturn that began in 1929, communist ideas spread throughout Iraq and the party slowly developed in coherence and ideology throughout the 1930s.

Islam: a religion founded in the early seventh century C.E. in what is today western Saudi Arabia. Islam is one of the great monotheistic religions that emerged from the Middle East. Over time, it has spread throughout the globe to now include over 1.5 billion followers, known as Muslims.

Islamic Dawa Party: a Shi'i political group founded in Iraq in 1957 as a response to ascendant secular ideologies such as Ba'thism. In the 1970s, the party waged an armed insurgency against the Ba'thist regime, and attempted to assassinate Saddam Hussein twice in the 1980s.

Islamic Revolution (1979): sometimes referred to as the Iranian Revolution, the revolution entailed the overthrow of the Pahlavi monarchy and its eventual replacement by an Islamic republic under the guidance of prominent Shi'i clerics.

Islamic State: an extremist group that began as a terrorist cell undertaking attacks in Iraq in the wake of the American invasion in 2003. In 2014, the group claimed large swathes of territory in Syria and Iraq.

Israel: a modern state founded in 1948 after the failure of a United Nations partition plan for the British Mandate of Palestine. The country is located at the eastern end of the Mediterranean Sea with its capital Jerusalem.

Jordan: a modern state that came into existence at the end of World War I as the British Mandate of Transjordan. The country is landlocked, bordered by Syria to the north, Iraq to the east, Israel and the Palestinian territories to the west, and Saudi Arabia to the south.

Lebanon: a modern state created from a special territory under nominal Ottoman control known as Mount Lebanon. The state came into its current shape after World War I, when the French added territory to Lebanon under its mandate over Lebanon and Syria.

Luddite: groups of early nineteenth-century English workers who sabotaged new machinery that threatened to make their labor obsolete. The term can also refer to any person opposed to new forms of technology.

Martial law: the suspension of ordinary laws in favor of government by the military.

Marxism: a view of history and a method of socio-political analysis. According to Marxism, capitalist societies are characterized by a conflict between socio-economic classes vying for control over wealth or production. Marxist analyses generally focus on the nature of the economic system, the formation of classes, and the conflicts that arise as a result of wealth distribution.

Medieval period: also known as the Middle Ages, and generally considered to last from the fifth to the fifteenth century. It is so called as it is the middle of the three common divisions in history: antiquity, the middle ages, and the modern period.

Modernization theory: a concept that seeks to identify the steps or parameters necessary for less-developed societies to attain the same level of social and economic progress as developed societies.

Nationalism: a political ideology centered around the idea that an individual belongs to a particular nation.

New social history: The new social history came to the fore in the 1960s and 1970s. It is a branch of historical analysis that focuses on the experiences of ordinary people, rather than the actions and motivations of the elite. New social histories include analyses of labor, women and gender, family, class and education, among others.

Ottoman Empire: a large continental empire established by Turkic tribes in Anatolia in 1299 that eventually grew to cover large parts of southeastern Europe, Western Asia, and North Africa. The Empire was dissolved in the aftermath of World War I.

Palestine: a term that has a longer history, though its twentieth-century usage mainly refers to the British Mandate of Palestine, when a region between the Mediterranean Sea and the Jordan River moved from Ottoman control to British. The British ruled Palestine from 1920 to 1948.

Paris Peace Conference (1919): took place at the conclusion of World War I and set the terms for the ending of military hostilities between the major Allied Powers (the United States, Great Britain, France, and Italy) and the Central Powers (Germany, Austria-Hungary, and the Ottoman Empire).

Political Islam: also known as "Islamism," refers to a range of ideologies positing an active political identity based on religious belief.

Political Islam is a controversial term and may best be understood as referring to a range of ideas regarding the role of religious belief and practice in the public political sphere.

Russian Revolution (1917): involved a series of upheavals that ended the tsarist monarchy and brought a socialist party to power, eventually leading to the establishment of the Union of Soviet Socialist Republics (USSR) in 1922.

September 1970 civil war: also known as Black September, this civil war pitted armed elements of the Palestine Liberation Organization against the Jordanian Armed Forces and the country's monarchy. The civil war ended in July 1971 with a victory for the Jordanian monarch.

Shi'i Islam: the second largest sect of Islam (after Sunni) is itself divided among three main branches. Shi'i Muslims are known as "the party of Ali" and believe that the Prophet Muhammad's religious authority passed to his descendants through his son-in-law, 'Ali ibn Abi Talib. Shi'i Muslims make up approximately 10–15 percent of the total Muslim population.

Socialism: an idea stemming from Marxist economic theory, which posits the co-operative ownership of property and the direction of economic enterprise towards the satisfaction of human needs.

Socio-economic classes: refers to a category of analysis whereby individuals are categorized based on social and economic background. According to Marx, the concept is fundamentally connected to a given individual's relationship to the means of production.

Sociologist: a person who studies sociology, the scientific investigation of society.

Soviet Union: the Union of Soviet Socialist Republics, often shortened to "Soviet Union," had its roots in the Russian Revolution of 1917, which overthrew the tsarist regime of the Russian Empire. In 1922, a communist regime led by Vladimir Lenin established the Soviet Union after prevailing in a military conflict against anti-revolution parties.

Structuralism: a social paradigm popularized in France in the early twentieth century, which asserts that there is an underlying architecture to human activities, a system of interrelations that may be discerned and described.

Suez Crisis (1956): occurred as a result of Egyptian president Gamal Abdel Nasser's attempt to assert Egyptian sovereignty over the Suez Canal, which runs through Egyptian territory connecting the Red Sea to the Mediterranean. As a response to Egypt's nationalization of the canal company in 1956, Israel, France, and Britain invaded the country. They were later forced to withdraw from Egypt under intense pressure from the Soviet Union and the United States.

Superpower: a nation-state capable of exerting power and influence in international relations at a global scale.

Supreme Council for the Islamic Revolution in Iraq: a Shi'i Islamist political party dedicated to overthrowing the Ba'thist regime of Saddam Hussein. It was founded in 1982 during the Iraq–Iran war, competed in elections in Iraq after the American invasion, and later changed its name to the Islamic Supreme Council of Iraq.

Transjordan: see Jordan.

World War I (1914–18): a global conflict pitting the Allies, a group of countries including the United Kingdom, France, and Russia, against the Central Powers, which included Germany, Austria–Hungary, and the Ottoman Empire. The United States entered the conflict in 1917. The war ended with the defeat of the Central Powers.

World War II (1939–45): started as a European conflict between Germany and her neighbors, which resulted in the eruption of tensions around the world. The United States entered the conflict in 1941. The war ended with the defeat of Germany and her allies and the dropping of atomic weapons on Hiroshima and Nagasaki in Japan. About 50 million people died before the war was brought to an end.

PEOPLE MENTIONED IN THE TEXT

Ervand Abrahamian (b. 1940) is distinguished professor of history at Baruch College, City University of New York. He has written extensively on the history of Iran.

Abd ar-Rahman Arif (1916–2007) was the president of Iraq from 1966 to 1968. He was overthrown in a Ba'th Party coup and spent 11 years in exile living in Istanbul before he was allowed to return to Iraq.

Orit Bashkin (b. 1974) is professor of modern Middle Eastern history at the University of Chicago. Her research interests include gender history, intellectual history, and Jewish history.

Joel Beinin (b. 1948) is a social historian and professor at Stanford University. He has also served as the director of Middle East studies at the American University in Cairo. His research focuses on workers and minorities in the modern Middle East.

Arbella Bet-Shlimon is an assistant professor at the University of Washington. Her research focuses on the politics, society, and economy of twentieth-century Iraq.

James A. Bill is Wendy and Emery Reves Professor Emeritus of International Studies for the Department of Government at William and Mary College. His research focuses on international politics with special attention to Middle East affairs.

Harold Bowen (1896–1959) served in the British Diplomatic Service in the Middle East during World War II. From 1951 until his death in 1959, he was reader in history at the School of Oriental and African Studies, University of London.

Dwight D. Eisenhower (1890–1969) was the 34th president of the United States of America from 1953 to 1961. He was also a five-star general and the supreme allied commander of the Allied Forces in Europe.

Marion Farouk-Sluglett (1936–96) was adjunct associate professor of political science at the University of Utah. She was well known internationally for her work on contemporary Iraq and on other aspects of modern Middle Eastern history.

Johan Franzén completed his PhD in modern Middle Eastern history at the School of Oriental and African Studies, University of London. He is currently a senior lecturer at the University of East Anglia.

Sir Hamilton Alexander Rosskeen Gibb (1895–1971) was born in Alexandria, Egypt. He was an historian, linguist, and orientalist. He was Laudian Professor of Arabic at St. John's College, Oxford, for 18 years and in 1955 he became professor of Arabic at Harvard University.

Samira Haj (b. 1945) is a professor of history at the College of Staten Island, City University of New York. Her research interests include the Middle East, Iraq, Islam, and modernity.

Albert Hourani (1915–93) was born in Manchester, England to two immigrants from what is today southern Lebanon. He taught at Magdalen College, Oxford University, and wrote extensively on Middle Eastern history.

Eric Hobsbawm (1917–2012) was a British historian born in Egypt. He served as the president of Birkbeck College, University of London from 2002 to 2012. His research focused on empire and capitalism in the nineteenth century.

Saddam Hussein (Abd al-Majid al-Tikriti) (1937–2006) was the fifth president of Iraq, from 16 July 1979 until 9 April 2003. As one of the leaders of the Ba'th Party he helped to bring about the coup of 1968 that restored the party to power. He fought two wars against the United States and was convicted of war crimes and subsequently executed.

Tareq Y. Ismael is a professor of political science at the University of Calgary and editor of the *International Journal of Contemporary Iraqi Studies*. He has written two books on communism in the Middle East.

Hashim Jawad (1911–1969) was a Sunni Arab of Baghdad. He was Iraq's representative at the United Nations prior to the 1958 revolution and then served as the foreign minister of Iraq from 1959 to 1963.

Abd ar-Rahman al-Kawakibi (1855–1902) was a Syrian intellectual and author. He was a critic of Ottoman governance and a supporter of pan-Arabism.

Abbas Kelidar (b. 1936) is a former professor of politics and history at the School of Oriental and African Studies, University of London. His research focuses on modern Iraq.

George Kennan (1904–2005) was an American historian and diplomat. His writings on international relations inspired American policies of "containment" of the Soviet Union during the Cold War.

Rashid Khalidi (b. 1948) is an Oxford University-educated American historian of the Middle East and editor of the *Journal of Palestine Studies*. He is currently the Edward Said Professor of Modern Arab Studies at Columbia University.

Philip Khoury (b. 1949) is Ford International Professor of History at the Massachusetts Institute of Technology. He has written several books on the Middle East, mainly focusing on Syria and Lebanon.

Walter Laqueur (b. 1921) is an American historian. He was University Professor at Georgetown University from 1976 to 1988. He has written many books, including several Cold War studies of the Middle East.

Bernard Lewis (b. 1916) is an historian of Islamic and Middle Eastern studies and political commentator. He taught at the School of Oriental and African Studies, University of London, for over 30 years and has published widely.

John Locke (1632–1704) was an English philosopher. His writings were influential in the field of political philosophy, particularly with respect to British empiricism and classical liberalism.

Zachary Lockman (b. 1952) is a professor of history at New York University. He writes and teaches about the socio-economic and political history of the modern Middle East.

William Roger Louis (b. 1936) is a historian of the British Empire. He is a professor at the University of Texas at Austin and a past president of the American Historical Association.

Pierre-Jean Luizard (b. 1954) is the director of the French Centre National de la Recherche Scientifique (CNRS) in Paris. He is a historian of contemporary Islam and has published works on Iraq, Iran, and Egypt.

James Madison (1751–1836) was an American political philosopher and statesman. He was the fourth president of the United States of America, from 1809 to 1817.

Karl Marx (1818–83) was a nineteenth-century German intellectual. His writings on labor and capital had a long-lasting influence on economic thought and gave rise to communism, a political theory and economic ideology that advocates the collective ownership of property and social revolution ending in a classless society.

Yitzhak Nakash (b. 1958) is Associate Professor of Middle East History and Chair of the Program of Islamic and Middle Eastern Studies at Brandeis University. He has published extensively on Shi'a Islam and Shi'a communities in the Middle East.

Gamal Abdel Nasser (1918–70) was a leading figure in the Egyptian Free Officers Movement and the second President of Egypt from 1956 until his death in 1970.

Edward Roger Owen (b. 1935) is a British historian who is currently A. J. Meyer Professor Emeritus of Middle East History at Harvard. He has written extensively on the economic history of the region, with a special emphasis on Egypt.

Mohammed Reza Pahlavi (1919–80) was the Shah (King) of Iran from September 1941 until he was overthrown by a popular uprising in February 1979. He died of cancer in 1980.

Sara Pursley is a fellow at Princeton University's Society of Fellows and in 2016 will join the New York University faculty as an assistant professor of modern Middle East history. Her research focuses on the cultural and social history of Iraq.

Abd al-Karim Qasim (1914–63) was a general in the Iraqi army who overthrew the Iraqi monarchy and seized power in 1958. He became Prime Minister of the new Republic of Iraq and ruled until the 1963 Ba'thist revolution, whereupon he was deposed and executed.

Joseph Sassoon was born in Baghdad and is an independent academic based in London. He is a senior associate member of St Antony's College, Oxford University. He is the author of numerous books on the Iraqi economy and the Middle East region.

Edward Said (1935–2005) was an American of Palestinian descent who pioneered the field of postcolonial theory. He was professor of English and comparative literature at Columbia University and published extensively on topics related to the Middle East.

Priya Satia is associate professor of modern British history at Stanford University. She has written on the cultural history of the British Empire in the Middle East and South Asia.

Peter John Sluglett (b. 1943) is a British-born historian of the nineteenth- and twentieth-century Arab Middle East who has written extensively on Iraq. He is a professor at the University of Utah and has published widely on Iraq.

Joe Stork is deputy director of the Middle East and North Africa division of Human Rights Watch. He co-founded the Middle East

Research and Information Project (MERIP) and has written extensively about Middle Eastern affairs.

Edward Palmer Thompson (1924–93) was a British historian who studied at the University of Cambridge. He founded the Communist Party Historians Group in 1946 and the influential journal *Past and Present* in 1952.

Charles Townshend (b. 1945) is professor of international history at Keele University in the United Kingdom. He has written about the role of British imperialism in Ireland and Palestine.

Charles Tripp (b. 1952) is professor of politics at the School of Oriental and African Studies, University of London. He specializes in the history and politics of the Middle East.

Max Weber (1864–1920) was a German social theorist who published important works of social theory during the late nineteenth century. His writings were critical to the founding of the new academic discipline of sociology.

Mary C. Wilson is professor of history at the University of Massachusetts. Her research focuses on Jordan and Syria.

WORKS CITED

WORKS CITED

Abrahamian, Ervand. *Iran between Two Revolutions*. Princeton, NJ: Princeton University Press, 1982.

Arjomand, Said Amir. Review of *The Old Social Classes and the Revolutionary Movements of Iraq: A Study of Iraq's Old Landed and Commercial Classes and of Its Communists, Ba'thists, and Free Officers*, by Hanna Batatu. *American Journal of Sociology* 88 (1982): 469–71.

Barnes, Bart. "Scholar Hanna Batatu, 74, Dies; Authority on Modern Iraq, Syria." *Washington Post*, June 28, 2000.

Bashkin, Orit. *The Other Iraq: Pluralism and Culture in Hashemite Iraq*. Stanford, CA: Stanford University Press, 2009.

Batatu, Hanna. "Of the Diversity of Iraqis, the Incohesiveness of their Society, and their Progress in the Monarchic Period toward a Consolidated Political Structure." In *The Modern Middle East*, edited by Albert Hourani, Philip Khoury, and Mary C. Wilson, 503–25. London: I.B. Tauris, 2004.

The Egyptian, Syrian, and Iraqi Revolutions: Some Observations on Their Underlying Causes and Social Character. Washington, DC: Georgetown University Press, 1984.

"The Old Social Classes Revisited." In *The Iraqi Revolution of 1958: The Old Social Classes Revisited*, edited by Robert A. Fernea and W. Roger Louis, 211–22. London: I.B. Tauris, 1991.

The Old Social Classes and the Revolutionary Movements of Iraq: A Study of Iraq's Landed and Commercial Classes and of its Communists, Ba'thists and Free Officers. Princeton, NJ: Princeton University Press, 1978.

 Syria's Peasantry, the Descendants of Its Lesser Rural Notables, and Their Politics. Princeton, NJ: Princeton University Press, 1999.

Batatu, Hanna, and Philip Khoury and Joe Stork. "Hanna Batatu's Achievement: A Faithful History of the Class Struggle in Iraq." *MERIP Reports* 97 (1981): 22–32.Beinin, Joel. "Class and Politics in Middle Eastern Societies. A Review Article." *Comparative Studies in Society and History* 28, no. 3 (1986): 552–7.

Beinin, Joel, and Zachary Lockman. *Workers on the Nile: Nationalism, Communism, Islam and the Egyptian Working Class, 1882–1954.* Princeton, NJ: Princeton University Press, 1987.

Bet-Shlimon, Arbella. "Group Identities, Oil, and the Local Political Domain in Kirkuk: A Historical Perspective." *Journal of Urban History* 38 (2012): 914–31.

Bill, James A. Review of *The Old Social Classes and the Revolutionary*
Movements of Iraq: A Study of Iraq's Old Landed and Commercial Classes and
of its Communists, Ba'thists and Free Officers, by Hanna Batatu. *American*
Political Science Review 74 (1980): 529–30.

Davis, Diana K. *Resurrecting the Granary of Rome: Environmental History and*
French Colonial Expansion in North Africa. Athens, OH: Ohio University Press,
2007.

Dodge, Toby. *Inventing Iraq: The Failure of Nation Building and a History Denied*.
New York: Columbia University Press, 2003.

Eisenhower, Dwight D. "Special Message to the Congress on the Situation
in the Middle East," January 5, 1957. Online by Gerhard Peters and John T.
Woolley. *The American Presidency Project*. Accessed February 23, 2015. www.
presidency.ucsb.edu/ws/?pid=11007.

Elliot, Matthew. *'Independent Iraq': The Monarchy and British Influence, 1941–*
1958. London: Tauris Academic Studies, 1996.

Farouk-Sluglett, Marion, and Peter Sluglett. Review of "Book II: The Communists
and Their Movement." In *The Old Social Classes and the Revolutionary*
Movements of Iraq: A Study of Iraq's Landed and Commercial Classes and of its
Communists, Ba'thists and Free Officers, by Hanna Batatu. *MERIP Reports* 97
(1981): 27.

"The Social Classes and the Origins of the Revolution." In *The Iraqi Revolution*
of 1958: The Old Social Classes Revisited, edited by Robert A. Fernea and Wm.
Roger Louis. London: I.B. Tauris, 1991.

Fernea, Robert A., and Wm. Roger Louis, eds. *The Iraqi Revolution of 1958: The*
Old Social Classes Revisited. London: I.B. Tauris, 1991.

Franzén, Johan. *Red Star Over Iraq: The Iraqi Communist Party and the Evolution*
of Ideological Politics in Pre-Saddam Iraq. New York: Columbia University Press,
2011.

Gibb, H. A. R., and Harold Bowen. *Islamic Society and the West: A Study of the*
Impact of Western Civilization on Moslem Culture in the Near East. London:
Oxford University Press, 1950.

Haj, Samira. *The Making of Iraq, 1900–1963: Capital, Power, and Ideology*.
Albany, NY: SUNY Press, 1997.

Harlow, Giles D., and George C. Maerz, eds. *Measures Short of War:*
The George F. Kennan Lectures at the National War College 1946–1947.
Washington, DC: National Defense University Press, 1991.

Hobsbawm, Eric. "The Revival of Narrative: Some Comments." *Past & Present*
86 (1980): 3–8.

Horowitz, Tony. *Baghdad Without a Map and Other Misadventures in Arabia*. New York: Plume, 1991.

Hourani, Albert, Philip Khoury, and Mary C. Wilson, eds. *The Modern Middle East: A Reader*. London: I.B. Tauris, 2005.

İslamoğlu, Huri and Çağlar Keyder. "Agenda for Ottoman History." In *The Ottoman Empire and the World-Economy*, edited by Huri İslamoğlu-İnan, 42–62. Cambridge: Cambridge University Press, 1987.

Ismael, Tareq Y. *The Rise and Fall of the Communist Party of Iraq*. New York: Cambridge University Press, 2008.

Jacobs, Matthew F. *Imagining the Middle East: The Building of an American Foreign Policy, 1918–1967*. Chapel Hill, NC: UNC Press, 2011.

Johnson, Paul E. "Looking Back at Social History." *Reviews in American History* 39 (2011): 379–88.

Kelidar, Abbas. Review of *The Old Social Classes and the Revolutionary Movements of Iraq: A Study of Iraq's Old Landed and Commercial Classes and of its Communists, Ba'thists and Free Officers*, by Hanna Batatu. *International Affairs* 56 (1980): 741–2.

Khadduri, Majid. *Independent Iraq: A Study in Iraqi Politics since 1932*. London: Oxford University Press, 1951.

Republican Iraq: A Study in Iraqi Politics Since the Revolution of 1958. London: Oxford University Press, 1969.

Socialist Iraq: A Study in Iraqi Politics Since 1968. Washington, DC: Middle East Institute, 1978.

Khalidi, Rashid. "The Impact of the Iraqi Revolution on the Arab World." In *The Iraqi Revolution of 1958: The Old Social Classes Revisited*, edited by Robert A. Fernea and W. Roger Louis, 106–117. London: I.B. Tauris, 1991.Laqueur, Walter. *Communism and Nationalism in the Middle East*. London: Routledge & Kegan Paul, 1956.

Lerner, Daniel. *The Passing of Traditional Society: Modernizing the Middle East*. New York: Free Press, 1958.

Lewis, Bernard. *The Emergence of Modern Turkey*. London: Oxford University Press, 1968.

Lipset, Seymour Martin. "Some Social Requisites of Democracy: Economic Development and Political Legitimacy." *American Political Science Review* 53 (1959): 69–105.

Longrigg, Stephen Hemsley. *Four Centuries of Modern Iraq*. Oxford: Clarendon Press, 1925.

Louis, Wm. Roger. "The British and the Origins of the Iraqi Revolution." In *The Iraqi Revolution of 1958: The Old Social Classes Revisited*, edited by Robert A. Fernea and W. Roger Louis, 31–61. London: I.B. Tauris, 1991.

Luizard, Pierre-Jean. *La Formation de l'Irak Contemporain: le Rôle Politique des Ulémas Chiites à la Fin de la Domination Ottomane et au Moment de la Construction de l'Etat Irakien.* Paris: Editions du Centre National de la Recherche Scientifique, 1991.

Marx, Karl. *Capital*. Edited by Frederick Engels. London: Swan Sonnenschein, Lowry and Co., 1887.

A Contribution to the Critique of Political Economy. Moscow: Progress Publishers, 1977.

Marx, Karl, and Frederick Engels. *Manifesto of the Communist Party*. Translated by Samuel Moore. London: William Reeves, 1888.

Mitchell, Timothy. *Carbon Democracy: Political Power in the Age of Oil*. New York: Verso, 2011.

Nakash, Yitzhak. *The Shi'is of Iraq*. Princeton, NJ: Princeton University Press, 1994.

Nieuwenhuis, Tom. Review of "Book 1: The Old Social Classes." In *The Old Social Classes and the Revolutionary Movements of Iraq: A Study of Iraq's Old Landed and Commercial Classes and of its Communists, Ba'thists and Free Officers*, by Hanna Batatu. *MERIP Reports* 97 (1981): 22, 24–5.

Owen, Roger. "Class and Class Politics in Iraq before 1958: The 'Colonial and Post-Colonial State'." In *The Iraqi Revolution of 1958: The Old Social Classes Revisited*, edited by Robert A. Fernea and W. Roger Louis, 154–71. London: I.B. Tauris, 1991.

"The Historian as Witness: In Memory of Hanna Batatu (1926–2000)." *Harvard Middle Eastern and Islamic Review* 6 (2000–2001): 94–107.

State, Power and Politics in the Making of the Modern Middle East. London: Routledge, 1992.

Polk, William R., and Richard L. Chambers, *Beginnings of Modernization in the Middle East: The Nineteenth Century*. Chicago: University of Chicago Press, 1968.

Pursley, Sara. "Daughters of the Right Path: Family Law, Homosocial Publics, and the Ethics of Intimacy in the Works of Shi'i Revivalist Bint al-Huda." *Journal of Middle East Women's Studies* 8 (2012): 51–77

Rosen, Nir. *Aftermath: Following the Bloodshed of America's Wars in the Muslim World.* New York: Nation Books, 2010.

Said, Edward. *Orientalism*. New York: Vintage Books, 1979.

Sassoon, Joseph. *Saddam Hussein's Ba'th Party: Inside an Authoritarian Regime*. Cambridge: Cambridge University Press, 2012.

Satia, Priya. *Spies in Arabia: The Great War and the Cultural Foundations of Britain's Covert Empire in the Middle East*. New York: Oxford University Press, 2008.

Simon, Reeva Spector. *Iraq Between the Two World Wars: The Militarist Origins of Tyranny*. New York: Columbia University Press, 1986.

Sluglett, Peter. *Britain in Iraq, 1914–1932*. London: Ithaca Press, 1976.

"Hanna Batatu and Iraqi Politics." *Democratiya* 4 (2006): 7–19.

Stepan, Alfred, and Graeme B. Robertson. "An 'Arab' More than 'Muslim' Electoral Gap." *Journal of Democracy* 14 (2003): 30–44.

Stork, Joe. Review of "Book III: The Communists, Ba'thists and Free Officers." In *The Old Social Classes and the Revolutionary Movements of Iraq: A Study of Iraq's Old Landed and Commercial Classes and of its Communists, Ba'thists and Free Officers*, by Hanna Batatu. *MERIP Reports* 97 (1981): 23–32.

Thompson, E. P. *The Making of the English Working Class*. London: Victor Gollancz, 1980.

Townshend, Charles. *Desert Hell: The British Invasion of Mesopotamia*. Cambridge: Belknap Press, 2010.

Tripp, Charles. *A History of Iraq*. Cambridge: Cambridge University Press, 2000.

Vesey, Laurence. "The 'New' Social History in the Context of American Historical Writing." *Reviews in American History* 7 (1979): 1–12.

Waterbury, John. "Democracy without Democrats?" In *Democracy without Democrats? The Renewal of Politics in the Muslim World,* edited by Ghassan Salamé, 23–47. London: I.B. Tauris, 1994.

Weber, Max. *Economy and Society*. Edited by Guenther Roth and Claus Wittich. Berkeley, CA: University of California Press, 1978.

THE MACAT LIBRARY
BY DISCIPLINE

AFRICANA STUDIES

Chinua Achebe's *An Image of Africa: Racism in Conrad's Heart of Darkness*
W. E. B. Du Bois's *The Souls of Black Folk*
Zora Neale Huston's *Characteristics of Negro Expression*
Martin Luther King Jr's *Why We Can't Wait*
Toni Morrison's *Playing in the Dark: Whiteness in the American Literary Imagination*

ANTHROPOLOGY

Arjun Appadurai's *Modernity at Large: Cultural Dimensions of Globalisation*
Philippe Ariès's *Centuries of Childhood*
Franz Boas's *Race, Language and Culture*
Kim Chan & Renée Mauborgne's *Blue Ocean Strategy*
Jared Diamond's *Guns, Germs & Steel: the Fate of Human Societies*
Jared Diamond's *Collapse: How Societies Choose to Fail or Survive*
E. E. Evans-Pritchard's *Witchcraft, Oracles and Magic Among the Azande*
James Ferguson's *The Anti-Politics Machine*
Clifford Geertz's *The Interpretation of Cultures*
David Graeber's *Debt: the First 5000 Years*
Karen Ho's *Liquidated: An Ethnography of Wall Street*
Geert Hofstede's *Culture's Consequences: Comparing Values, Behaviors, Institutes and Organizations across Nations*
Claude Lévi-Strauss's *Structural Anthropology*
Jay Macleod's *Ain't No Makin' It: Aspirations and Attainment in a Low-Income Neighborhood*
Saba Mahmood's *The Politics of Piety: The Islamic Revival and the Feminist Subjec*t
Marcel Mauss's *The Gift*

BUSINESS

Jean Lave & Etienne Wenger's *Situated Learning*
Theodore Levitt's *Marketing Myopia*
Burton G. Malkiel's *A Random Walk Down Wall Street*
Douglas McGregor's *The Human Side of Enterprise*
Michael Porter's *Competitive Strategy: Creating and Sustaining Superior Performance*
John Kotter's *Leading Change*
C. K. Prahalad & Gary Hamel's *The Core Competence of the Corporation*

CRIMINOLOGY

Michelle Alexander's *The New Jim Crow: Mass Incarceration in the Age of Colorblindness*
Michael R. Gottfredson & Travis Hirschi's *A General Theory of Crime*
Richard Herrnstein & Charles A. Murray's *The Bell Curve: Intelligence and Class Structure in American Life*
Elizabeth Loftus's *Eyewitness Testimony*
Jay Macleod's *Ain't No Makin' It: Aspirations and Attainment in a Low-Income Neighborhood*
Philip Zimbardo's *The Lucifer Effect*

ECONOMICS

Janet Abu-Lughod's *Before European Hegemony*
Ha-Joon Chang's *Kicking Away the Ladder*
David Brion Davis's *The Problem of Slavery in the Age of Revolution*
Milton Friedman's *The Role of Monetary Policy*
Milton Friedman's *Capitalism and Freedom*
David Graeber's *Debt: the First 5000 Years*
Friedrich Hayek's *The Road to Serfdom*
Karen Ho's *Liquidated: An Ethnography of Wall Street*

John Maynard Keynes's *The General Theory of Employment, Interest and Money*
Charles P. Kindleberger's *Manias, Panics and Crashes*
Robert Lucas's *Why Doesn't Capital Flow from Rich to Poor Countries?*
Burton G. Malkiel's *A Random Walk Down Wall Street*
Thomas Robert Malthus's *An Essay on the Principle of Population*
Karl Marx's *Capital*
Thomas Piketty's *Capital in the Twenty-First Century*
Amartya Sen's *Development as Freedom*
Adam Smith's *The Wealth of Nations*
Nassim Nicholas Taleb's *The Black Swan: The Impact of the Highly Improbable*
Amos Tversky's & Daniel Kahneman's *Judgment under Uncertainty: Heuristics and Biases*
Mahbub Ul Haq's *Reflections on Human Development*
Max Weber's *The Protestant Ethic and the Spirit of Capitalism*

FEMINISM AND GENDER STUDIES

Judith Butler's *Gender Trouble*
Simone De Beauvoir's *The Second Sex*
Michel Foucault's *History of Sexuality*
Betty Friedan's *The Feminine Mystique*
Saba Mahmood's *The Politics of Piety: The Islamic Revival and the Feminist Subject*
Joan Wallach Scott's *Gender and the Politics of History*
Mary Wollstonecraft's *A Vindication of the Rights of Woman*
Virginia Woolf's *A Room of One's Own*

GEOGRAPHY

The Brundtland Report's *Our Common Future*
Rachel Carson's *Silent Spring*
Charles Darwin's *On the Origin of Species*
James Ferguson's *The Anti-Politics Machine*
Jane Jacobs's *The Death and Life of Great American Cities*
James Lovelock's *Gaia: A New Look at Life on Earth*
Amartya Sen's *Development as Freedom*
Mathis Wackernagel & William Rees's *Our Ecological Footprint*

HISTORY

Janet Abu-Lughod's *Before European Hegemony*
Benedict Anderson's *Imagined Communities*
Bernard Bailyn's *The Ideological Origins of the American Revolution*
Hanna Batatu's *The Old Social Classes And The Revolutionary Movements Of Iraq*
Christopher Browning's *Ordinary Men: Reserve Police Batallion 101 and the Final Solution in Poland*
Edmund Burke's *Reflections on the Revolution in France*
William Cronon's *Nature's Metropolis: Chicago And The Great West*
Alfred W. Crosby's *The Columbian Exchange*
Hamid Dabashi's *Iran: A People Interrupted*
David Brion Davis's *The Problem of Slavery in the Age of Revolution*
Nathalie Zemon Davis's *The Return of Martin Guerre*
Jared Diamond's *Guns, Germs & Steel: the Fate of Human Societies*
Frank Dikotter's *Mao's Great Famine*
John W Dower's *War Without Mercy: Race And Power In The Pacific War*
W. E. B. Du Bois's *The Souls of Black Folk*
Richard J. Evans's *In Defence of History*
Lucien Febvre's *The Problem of Unbelief in the 16th Century*
Sheila Fitzpatrick's *Everyday Stalinism*

Eric Foner's *Reconstruction: America's Unfinished Revolution, 1863-1877*
Michel Foucault's *Discipline and Punish*
Michel Foucault's *History of Sexuality*
Francis Fukuyama's *The End of History and the Last Man*
John Lewis Gaddis's *We Now Know: Rethinking Cold War History*
Ernest Gellner's *Nations and Nationalism*
Eugene Genovese's *Roll, Jordan, Roll: The World the Slaves Made*
Carlo Ginzburg's *The Night Battles*
Daniel Goldhagen's *Hitler's Willing Executioners*
Jack Goldstone's *Revolution and Rebellion in the Early Modern World*
Antonio Gramsci's *The Prison Notebooks*
Alexander Hamilton, John Jay & James Madison's *The Federalist Papers*
Christopher Hill's *The World Turned Upside Down*
Carole Hillenbrand's *The Crusades: Islamic Perspectives*
Thomas Hobbes's *Leviathan*
Eric Hobsbawm's *The Age Of Revolution*
John A. Hobson's *Imperialism: A Study*
Albert Hourani's *History of the Arab Peoples*
Samuel P. Huntington's *The Clash of Civilizations and the Remaking of World Order*
C. L. R. James's *The Black Jacobins*
Tony Judt's *Postwar: A History of Europe Since 1945*
Ernst Kantorowicz's *The King's Two Bodies: A Study in Medieval Political Theology*
Paul Kennedy's *The Rise and Fall of the Great Powers*
Ian Kershaw's *The "Hitler Myth": Image and Reality in the Third Reich*
John Maynard Keynes's *The General Theory of Employment, Interest and Money*
Charles P. Kindleberger's *Manias, Panics and Crashes*
Martin Luther King Jr's *Why We Can't Wait*
Henry Kissinger's *World Order: Reflections on the Character of Nations and the Course of History*
Thomas Kuhn's *The Structure of Scientific Revolutions*
Georges Lefebvre's *The Coming of the French Revolution*
John Locke's *Two Treatises of Government*
Niccolò Machiavelli's *The Prince*
Thomas Robert Malthus's *An Essay on the Principle of Population*
Mahmood Mamdani's *Citizen and Subject: Contemporary Africa And The Legacy Of Late Colonialism*
Karl Marx's *Capital*
Stanley Milgram's *Obedience to Authority*
John Stuart Mill's *On Liberty*
Thomas Paine's *Common Sense*
Thomas Paine's *Rights of Man*
Geoffrey Parker's *Global Crisis: War, Climate Change and Catastrophe in the Seventeenth Century*
Jonathan Riley-Smith's *The First Crusade and the Idea of Crusading*
Jean-Jacques Rousseau's *The Social Contract*
Joan Wallach Scott's *Gender and the Politics of History*
Theda Skocpol's *States and Social Revolutions*
Adam Smith's *The Wealth of Nations*
Timothy Snyder's *Bloodlands: Europe Between Hitler and Stalin*
Sun Tzu's *The Art of War*
Keith Thomas's *Religion and the Decline of Magic*
Thucydides's *The History of the Peloponnesian War*
Frederick Jackson Turner's *The Significance of the Frontier in American History*
Odd Arne Westad's *The Global Cold War: Third World Interventions And The Making Of Our Times*

The Macat Library By Discipline

LITERATURE

Chinua Achebe's *An Image of Africa: Racism in Conrad's Heart of Darkness*
Roland Barthes's *Mythologies*
Homi K. Bhabha's *The Location of Culture*
Judith Butler's *Gender Trouble*
Simone De Beauvoir's *The Second Sex*
Ferdinand De Saussure's *Course in General Linguistics*
T. S. Eliot's *The Sacred Wood: Essays on Poetry and Criticism*
Zora Neale Huston's *Characteristics of Negro Expression*
Toni Morrison's *Playing in the Dark: Whiteness in the American Literary Imagination*
Edward Said's *Orientalism*
Gayatri Chakravorty Spivak's *Can the Subaltern Speak?*
Mary Wollstonecraft's *A Vindication of the Rights of Women*
Virginia Woolf's *A Room of One's Own*

PHILOSOPHY

Elizabeth Anscombe's *Modern Moral Philosophy*
Hannah Arendt's *The Human Condition*
Aristotle's *Metaphysics*
Aristotle's *Nicomachean Ethics*
Edmund Gettier's *Is Justified True Belief Knowledge?*
Georg Wilhelm Friedrich Hegel's *Phenomenology of Spirit*
David Hume's *Dialogues Concerning Natural Religion*
David Hume's *The Enquiry for Human Understanding*
Immanuel Kant's *Religion within the Boundaries of Mere Reason*
Immanuel Kant's *Critique of Pure Reason*
Søren Kierkegaard's *The Sickness Unto Death*
Søren Kierkegaard's *Fear and Trembling*
C. S. Lewis's *The Abolition of Man*
Alasdair MacIntyre's *After Virtue*
Marcus Aurelius's *Meditations*
Friedrich Nietzsche's *On the Genealogy of Morality*
Friedrich Nietzsche's *Beyond Good and Evil*
Plato's *Republic*
Plato's *Symposium*
Jean-Jacques Rousseau's *The Social Contract*
Gilbert Ryle's *The Concept of Mind*
Baruch Spinoza's *Ethics*
Sun Tzu's *The Art of War*
Ludwig Wittgenstein's *Philosophical Investigations*

POLITICS

Benedict Anderson's *Imagined Communities*
Aristotle's *Politics*
Bernard Bailyn's *The Ideological Origins of the American Revolution*
Edmund Burke's *Reflections on the Revolution in France*
John C. Calhoun's *A Disquisition on Government*
Ha-Joon Chang's *Kicking Away the Ladder*
Hamid Dabashi's *Iran: A People Interrupted*
Hamid Dabashi's *Theology of Discontent: The Ideological Foundation of the Islamic Revolution in Iran*
Robert Dahl's *Democracy and its Critics*
Robert Dahl's *Who Governs?*
David Brion Davis's *The Problem of Slavery in the Age of Revolution*

Alexis De Tocqueville's *Democracy in America*
James Ferguson's *The Anti-Politics Machine*
Frank Dikotter's *Mao's Great Famine*
Sheila Fitzpatrick's *Everyday Stalinism*
Eric Foner's *Reconstruction: America's Unfinished Revolution, 1863-1877*
Milton Friedman's *Capitalism and Freedom*
Francis Fukuyama's *The End of History and the Last Man*
John Lewis Gaddis's *We Now Know: Rethinking Cold War History*
Ernest Gellner's *Nations and Nationalism*
David Graeber's *Debt: the First 5000 Years*
Antonio Gramsci's *The Prison Notebooks*
Alexander Hamilton, John Jay & James Madison's *The Federalist Papers*
Friedrich Hayek's *The Road to Serfdom*
Christopher Hill's *The World Turned Upside Down*
Thomas Hobbes's *Leviathan*
John A. Hobson's *Imperialism: A Study*
Samuel P. Huntington's *The Clash of Civilizations and the Remaking of World Order*
Tony Judt's *Postwar: A History of Europe Since 1945*
David C. Kang's *China Rising: Peace, Power and Order in East Asia*
Paul Kennedy's *The Rise and Fall of Great Powers*
Robert Keohane's *After Hegemony*
Martin Luther King Jr.'s *Why We Can't Wait*
Henry Kissinger's *World Order: Reflections on the Character of Nations and the Course of History*
John Locke's *Two Treatises of Government*
Niccolò Machiavelli's *The Prince*
Thomas Robert Malthus's *An Essay on the Principle of Population*
Mahmood Mamdani's *Citizen and Subject: Contemporary Africa And The Legacy Of Late Colonialism*
Karl Marx's *Capital*
John Stuart Mill's *On Liberty*
John Stuart Mill's *Utilitarianism*
Hans Morgenthau's *Politics Among Nations*
Thomas Paine's *Common Sense*
Thomas Paine's *Rights of Man*
Thomas Piketty's *Capital in the Twenty-First Century*
Robert D. Putman's *Bowling Alone*
John Rawls's *Theory of Justice*
Jean-Jacques Rousseau's *The Social Contract*
Theda Skocpol's *States and Social Revolutions*
Adam Smith's *The Wealth of Nations*
Sun Tzu's *The Art of War*
Henry David Thoreau's *Civil Disobedience*
Thucydides's *The History of the Peloponnesian War*
Kenneth Waltz's *Theory of International Politics*
Max Weber's *Politics as a Vocation*
Odd Arne Westad's *The Global Cold War: Third World Interventions And The Making Of Our Times*

POSTCOLONIAL STUDIES

Roland Barthes's *Mythologies*
Frantz Fanon's *Black Skin, White Masks*
Homi K. Bhabha's *The Location of Culture*
Gustavo Gutiérrez's *A Theology of Liberation*
Edward Said's *Orientalism*
Gayatri Chakravorty Spivak's *Can the Subaltern Speak?*

The Macat Library By Discipline

PSYCHOLOGY

Gordon Allport's *The Nature of Prejudice*
Alan Baddeley & Graham Hitch's *Aggression: A Social Learning Analysis*
Albert Bandura's *Aggression: A Social Learning Analysis*
Leon Festinger's *A Theory of Cognitive Dissonance*
Sigmund Freud's *The Interpretation of Dreams*
Betty Friedan's *The Feminine Mystique*
Michael R. Gottfredson & Travis Hirschi's *A General Theory of Crime*
Eric Hoffer's *The True Believer: Thoughts on the Nature of Mass Movements*
William James's *Principles of Psychology*
Elizabeth Loftus's *Eyewitness Testimony*
A. H. Maslow's *A Theory of Human Motivation*
Stanley Milgram's *Obedience to Authority*
Steven Pinker's *The Better Angels of Our Nature*
Oliver Sacks's *The Man Who Mistook His Wife For a Hat*
Richard Thaler & Cass Sunstein's *Nudge: Improving Decisions About Health, Wealth and Happiness*
Amos Tversky's *Judgment under Uncertainty: Heuristics and Biases*
Philip Zimbardo's *The Lucifer Effect*

SCIENCE

Rachel Carson's *Silent Spring*
William Cronon's *Nature's Metropolis: Chicago And The Great West*
Alfred W. Crosby's *The Columbian Exchange*
Charles Darwin's *On the Origin of Species*
Richard Dawkin's *The Selfish Gene*
Thomas Kuhn's *The Structure of Scientific Revolutions*
Geoffrey Parker's *Global Crisis: War, Climate Change and Catastrophe in the Seventeenth Century*
Mathis Wackernagel & William Rees's *Our Ecological Footprint*

SOCIOLOGY

Michelle Alexander's *The New Jim Crow: Mass Incarceration in the Age of Colorblindness*
Gordon Allport's *The Nature of Prejudice*
Albert Bandura's *Aggression: A Social Learning Analysis*
Hanna Batatu's *The Old Social Classes And The Revolutionary Movements Of Iraq*
Ha-Joon Chang's *Kicking Away the Ladder*
W. E. B. Du Bois's *The Souls of Black Folk*
Émile Durkheim's *On Suicide*
Frantz Fanon's *Black Skin, White Masks*
Frantz Fanon's *The Wretched of the Earth*
Eric Foner's *Reconstruction: America's Unfinished Revolution, 1863-1877*
Eugene Genovese's *Roll, Jordan, Roll: The World the Slaves Made*
Jack Goldstone's *Revolution and Rebellion in the Early Modern World*
Antonio Gramsci's *The Prison Notebooks*
Richard Herrnstein & Charles A Murray's *The Bell Curve: Intelligence and Class Structure in American Life*
Eric Hoffer's *The True Believer: Thoughts on the Nature of Mass Movements*
Jane Jacobs's *The Death and Life of Great American Cities*
Robert Lucas's *Why Doesn't Capital Flow from Rich to Poor Countries?*
Jay Macleod's *Ain't No Makin' It: Aspirations and Attainment in a Low Income Neighborhood*
Elaine May's *Homeward Bound: American Families in the Cold War Era*
Douglas McGregor's *The Human Side of Enterprise*
C. Wright Mills's *The Sociological Imagination*

Thomas Piketty's *Capital in the Twenty-First Century*
Robert D. Putman's *Bowling Alone*
David Riesman's *The Lonely Crowd: A Study of the Changing American Character*
Edward Said's *Orientalism*
Joan Wallach Scott's *Gender and the Politics of History*
Theda Skocpol's *States and Social Revolutions*
Max Weber's *The Protestant Ethic and the Spirit of Capitalism*

THEOLOGY

Augustine's *Confessions*
Benedict's *Rule of St Benedict*
Gustavo Gutiérrez's *A Theology of Liberation*
Carole Hillenbrand's *The Crusades: Islamic Perspectives*
David Hume's *Dialogues Concerning Natural Religion*
Immanuel Kant's *Religion within the Boundaries of Mere Reason*
Ernst Kantorowicz's *The King's Two Bodies: A Study in Medieval Political Theology*
Søren Kierkegaard's *The Sickness Unto Death*
C. S. Lewis's *The Abolition of Man*
Saba Mahmood's *The Politics of Piety: The Islamic Revival and the Feminist Subject*
Baruch Spinoza's *Ethics*
Keith Thomas's *Religion and the Decline of Magic*

COMING SOON

Chris Argyris's *The Individual and the Organisation*
Seyla Benhabib's *The Rights of Others*
Walter Benjamin's *The Work Of Art in the Age of Mechanical Reproduction*
John Berger's *Ways of Seeing*
Pierre Bourdieu's *Outline of a Theory of Practice*
Mary Douglas's *Purity and Danger*
Roland Dworkin's *Taking Rights Seriously*
James G. March's *Exploration and Exploitation in Organisational Learning*
Ikujiro Nonaka's *A Dynamic Theory of Organizational Knowledge Creation*
Griselda Pollock's *Vision and Difference*
Amartya Sen's *Inequality Re-Examined*
Susan Sontag's *On Photography*
Yasser Tabbaa's *The Transformation of Islamic Art*
Ludwig von Mises's *Theory of Money and Credit*

Printed in the United States
by Baker & Taylor Publisher Services